Mental Health Practice With Immigrant and Refugee Youth

Concise Guides on Trauma Care Series

Mental Health Practice With Immigrant and Refugee Youth

A Socioecological Framework

B. Heidi Ellis, Saida M. Abdi, and Jeffrey P. Winer

AMERICAN PSYCHOLOGICAL ASSOCIATION
Washington, DC

Published by
American Psychological Association
750 First Street, NE
Washington, DC 20002
https://www.apa.org
Order Department

https://www.apa.org/pubs/books
order@apa.org

In the U.K., Europe, Africa, and the Middle East, copies may be ordered from Eurospan
https://www.eurospanbookstore.com/apa
info@eurospangroup.com

Typeset in Charter by Circle Graphics, Inc., Reisterstown, MD

Printer: Sheridan Books, Chelsea, MI
Cover Designer: Mercury Publishing Services, Inc., Rockville, MD

Library of Congress Cataloging-in-Publication Data

Names: Ellis, Beverley Heidi, 1972- author. | Abdi, Saida M., author. |
    Winer, Jeffrey P., author.
Title: Mental health practice with immigrant and refugee youth :
    a socioecological framework / B. Heidi Ellis, Saida M. Abdi, Jeffrey P. Winer.
Description: Washington, DC : American Psychological Association, [2020] |
    Series: Concise guides on trauma care series | Includes bibliographical
    references and index.
Identifiers: LCCN 2019022629 (print) | LCCN 2019022630 (ebook) |
    ISBN 9781433831492 (paperback) | ISBN 9781433831737 (ebook)
Subjects: LCSH: Refugee children—Mental health—United States. |
    Refugee children—Mental health services—United States. | Immigrant
    youth—Mental health—United States. | Immigrant youth—Mental health
    services—United States. | Child mental health services—United States. |
    Cultural psychiatry.
Classification: LCC RJ507.R44 E45 2020 (print) | LCC RJ507.R44 (ebook) |
    DDC 362.2086/912—dc23
LC record available at https://lccn.loc.gov/2019022629
LC ebook record available at https://lccn.loc.gov/2019022630

http://dx.doi.org/10.1037/0000163-000

Printed in the United States of America

10 9 8 7 6 5 4 3 2 1

*To FK and TH, two of my early refugee clients who helped me
to understand the depth of human resilience
and the enduring capacity to love.*
—B. HEIDI ELLIS

*To the memory of my beloved Hooyo (mother),
Asha Sh. Mohamed Aw Mohamud, a refugee
whose courage and dedication is the reason
that I am able to do what I do today.*
—SAIDA M. ABDI

*For all the families of refugee and immigrant backgrounds
whom I've had the privilege to serve.*
—JEFFREY P. WINER

Contents

Series Foreword

Exposure to traumatic events is all too common, increasing the risk for a range of significant mental problems, such as posttraumatic stress disorder (PTSD) and depression; physical health problems; negative health behaviors, such as smoking and excessive alcohol consumption; impaired social and occupational functioning; and overall lower quality of life. As mass traumas (e.g., September 11, military engagements in Iraq and Afghanistan, natural disasters such as Hurricane Katrina) and public awareness/education campaigns (e.g., #metoo, Start by Believing) have propelled trauma into a brighter public spotlight, the number of trauma survivors seeking services for mental health consequences will likely continue to increase. Despite the far-ranging consequences of trauma and the high rates of exposure, relatively little emphasis is placed on trauma education in undergraduate and graduate training programs for mental health service providers in the United States. Calls for action have appeared in the American Psychological Association's journal *Psychological Trauma: Theory, Research, Practice, and Policy* with such articles as "The Need for Inclusion of Psychological Trauma in the Professional Curriculum: A Call to Action," by Christine A. Courtois and Steven N. Gold (2009) and "The Art and Science of Trauma-Focused Training and Education," by Anne P. DePrince and Elana Newman (2011). The lack of education in the assessment and treatment of trauma-related distress and associated clinical issues at undergraduate and graduate levels increases the urgency to develop effective trauma resources for students as well as postgraduate professionals.

This book series, Concise Guides on Trauma Care, addresses that urgent need by providing truly translational books that bring the best of trauma psychology science to mental health professions working in diverse settings. To do so, the series focuses on what we know (and do not know) about specific trauma topics, with attention to how trauma psychology science translates to diverse populations (diversity broadly defined, in terms of development, ethnicity, socioeconomic status, sexual orientation, and so forth).

This series represents one of many efforts undertaken by Division 56 (Trauma Psychology) of the American Psychological Association to advance trauma training and education (e.g., see https://www.apatraumadivision. org/68/teaching-training.html). We are pleased to work with Division 56 and a volunteer editorial board to develop this series, which continues to move forward with the publication of this important guide on mental health practice with immigrant and refugee youth by B. Heidi Ellis, Saida M. Abdi, and Jeffrey P. Winer. As immigrants and refugees continue to seek safe haven as a result of economic, political, and social unrest and prosecution in their home countries, this monograph offers a socioecological framework to better understand the plight of immigrants and refugees. The authors' discussions on working with refugee and immigrant families, including engagement, assessment, and treatment, will be of great use to mental health professionals as well as researchers and policy makers. Through case vignettes, the authors illustrate the importance of cultural considerations when working with refugees and immigrants. They also demonstrate ways to promote wellness and to rebuild resilient communities for families who have lost their support systems. Future books in the series will continue to address a range of assessment, treatment, and developmental issues in trauma-informed care.

—*Anne P. DePrince*
Ann T. Chu
Series Editors

Preface

"Tell me about one of the memories that stand out to you, from that time when you were traveling on your own. Maybe a memory that comes back to you the most." I was talking with a 15-year-old Ugandan girl, broaching the subject of a terribly painful time after her parents had been killed and she was desperately fleeing her village.[1] She had told me enough about her story for me to know that this was a period of her life marked by brutality and violence directed toward not only those she loved but herself as well. She paused, and I imagined she was reliving a terrible moment.

"The kindness of strangers," she said. "That's what I remember most. Like the time when I was going through a checkpoint: I had no money, and this stranger, he just ushered me through. He didn't know me; he didn't have to do that. I'm here because of the kindness of strangers."

Our work over the years with refugees and immigrants has been studded with moments like that one. We go into an encounter thinking it will be about one thing—about trauma, and loss perhaps—and come out having learned something else entirely; here resilience, and the power of human connection. It is this humbling recognition that we will never really be experts in the business of understanding humanity that makes it so compelling to try.

Working with refugees and immigrants offers a glimpse into both the worst and the best that humanity can be. To bear witness to the stories of

---

[1] Case material in this book has been disguised to protect client confidentiality.

people like this Ugandan girl is to confront the fact that people can and do perpetrate vile acts against children. We live in a time when it would be easy to be frozen by the sheer volume of atrocities that pervade our world. If we really try to make sense of the number of people who have been forced from their homes by war, conflict, poverty, and hatred, it becomes overwhelming and unreal. But it *is* real; it is the reality for millions of people throughout our world. What can we do in the face of such suffering?

We can do this: We can be strangers. We can be the strangers who show kindness. We can be the strangers who take an extra step to understand the child and family in front of us, who take on the task of helping them in the ways they most need. And perhaps, as the work unfolds, we will not be strangers anymore.

Acknowledgments

We gratefully acknowledge the many people over the course of our own journeys who have helped us to understand how we can help refugee and immigrant youth and families, and who have had a hand in shaping the ideas and content of this book. In particular, we thank our colleagues both past and present at the Refugee Trauma and Resilience Center at Boston Children's Hospital: Sarah Gillespie, who shepherded this manuscript through its development; Alisa Miller, Emma Cardeli, and Luna Mulder, who provided helpful comments on earlier drafts; and Osob Issa, Collen Bixby, Emily Hahn, and Molly Benson, for their work in shaping and supporting our center. We also thank Naima Agalab and the Refugee and Immigrant Assistance Center, who have partnered with us from the beginning in supporting our work and helping us understand communities and community engagement. We also thank our editors—Anne P. DePrince, Ann T. Chu, and Ted Baroody—for their encouragement, insights, and guidance throughout the writing; and the three reviewers who provided deeply thoughtful comments. Finally, we thank the youths themselves, who courageously shared their stories and healing journeys with us, so that we could share them with you.

Mental Health Practice With Immigrant and Refugee Youth

1

INTRODUCTION TO REFUGEES AND IMMIGRANTS

Newcomers to the United States

Today there are more refugees and forcibly displaced migrants than at any other time in history (United Nations High Commissioner for Refugees [UNHCR], 2018a). Global conflict and instability have led to mass migrations of people fleeing violence and brutality. Climate change threatens to make lands uninhabitable, adding to the global migration crisis. Globally, more than 68.5 million individuals have been forcibly displaced (UNHCR, 2018a); more than half of today's refugees are children under the age of 18 (UNHCR, 2018a). As they cross seas, lands, and ultimately borders seeking refuge, forcibly displaced migrants become stories in our newspapers and statistics in our political debates. But they are, more than anything else, individuals and families seeking a chance to survive and—ultimately—thrive.

Mental health providers may have the opportunity, for a brief period, to walk a part of the journey with refugee and immigrant children and families. That part of the journey may be soon after resettlement, as families struggle to make sense of their new land and challenges, or it may be a generation later, as a family grapples with questions of identity and historical trauma. Against the tapestry of political history, culture, violence, and flight that

http://dx.doi.org/10.1037/0000163-001
Mental Health Practice With Immigrant and Refugee Youth: A Socioecological Framework, by B. H. Ellis, S. M. Abdi, and J. P. Winer

weaves together the life experiences of refugees and immigrants, the therapeutic part of the journey may seem small and insignificant. However, it may also hold the potential to help children and families shift their journey toward one of greater hope, recovery, and resilience. This book is for mental health providers who may have this opportunity to work with refugees and immigrants or who would like to work to create this opportunity. Reading the chapters herein will provide frameworks to guide thinking around the needs and challenges of serving this population, as well as concrete steps to providing evidence-based, culturally responsive care. This book is also for providers from other disciplines who want to understand how culture, trauma, and mental health can shape the experiences of refugee and immigrant children. Finally, this book is for fellow citizens who, like us, believe we have a role in making our country a refuge and home to all who live here. Reading this book will provide a window into both the experiences and stories of refugee and immigrant children, as well as how the communities we build shape these stories.

This book explores the refugee or immigrant child's experience using a socioecological model (Bronfenbrenner, 1979; see Figure 1.1). Through this lens, the developing child is seen as being at the heart of a series of concentric

FIGURE 1.1. Socioecological Model Showing How the Individual Child Is Nested Within Layers of the Social Ecology

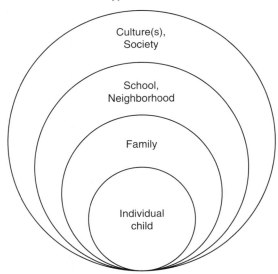

[handwritten margin note: disruptions at any layer affect child]

Different levels of the social ecology interact such that disruptions or interventions within one level of the ecology may affect functioning and stability of another level.

circles of the social ecology: He or she lives in a family, attends school, is part of a neighborhood and larger society, and all of this is embedded in a culture—or, for immigrants, both their culture of origin and the culture of their resettlement community. Disruptions in any one layer of this social ecology can have profound consequences for the developing child at its core. So, too, can assets—the gifts of family bonds, a teacher's warmth, a place on the town's soccer team. As we examine the evidence related to how trauma and stress impact a refugee child's development, we will also quickly move to understand how levers of intervention in the layers of the social ecology can reverse this impact and help foster resilience.

In this chapter, we describe what it means to be a refugee or forcibly displaced migrant, common experiences and challenges, and the diversity of outcomes that can be realized by the human spirit despite adversity. Chapter 2 provides an in-depth look at culture and how culture—both ours and those of our clients—is central to the relationship and work. Chapter 3 discusses barriers to engagement and practical strategies for overcoming them. Chapters 4 through 6 directly addresses working with refugee and immigrant children and adolescents, starting first with assessment, followed by office-based and trauma-focused approaches, and then collaborative or integrated approaches to care. Finally, Chapter 7 considers how resilient communities can positively shape the experience of refugees and immigrants, as well as what we need to do to build these communities.

TYPES OF IMMIGRANTS AND WHY IT MATTERS

Approximately 13.4% (43.2 million) of the U.S. population are immigrants (Pew Research Center, 2018). Depending on the legal determination made related to the circumstances of migration, immigrants may be refugees, asylum seekers, asylees, undocumented immigrants, unaccompanied children, unaccompanied refugee minors, or authorized immigrants. Understanding the legal standing of the child or family with whom a clinician works is important to recognizing what benefits they have access to and the stability of their residency. Some immigrants are voluntary migrants and migrate for reasons such as educational or professional opportunity or for family connection (American Psychological Association [APA] Presidential Task Force on Immigration, 2012). In contrast, some immigrants—including refugees, asylum seekers, and many undocumented immigrants—migrate in search of humanitarian refuge (APA Presidential Task Force on Immigration, 2012). These immigrants, who are forced to leave their home countries because of violence or political instability, not only share with other immigrants the challenges associated with acculturation but also must contend with stressors associated with the nonvoluntary nature of their migration. Although some of what is discussed in this book will be relevant for all immigrant children and families, the focus of this guide is on the particular needs of forced, or involuntary, migrants who come seeking refuge. Despite the diversity in cultures and journeys, some important common threads unite them all. (See Exhibit 1.1 and Table 1.1.)

Globally, there are 25.4 million refugees today, coming from regions around the world (UNHCR, 2018a). In 2017, the most frequent countries of origin included South Sudan, Afghanistan, and Syria, which together accounted for 57% of the world's displaced people (UNHCR, 2018a). They migrate where they can, and some receive formal resettlement opportunities in countries around the world. The term *refugee* is a formal legal status given by the UNHCR to an individual who, "owing to well-founded fear of being persecuted for reasons of race, religion, nationality, membership of a particular social group or political opinion, is outside the country of his nationality and is unable or, owing to such fear, is unwilling to avail himself of the protection of that country" (UNHCR, 1951). Typically, refugees flee from their homelands out of fear for their safety and find their way across country borders to a refugee camp, where they may wait indefinitely for conditions to allow them to return home or to be accepted for resettlement in another country.

Once resettled in the United States, refugees receive a one-time Reception and Placement Grant (RPG) that they can use to secure initial housing, food, or clothing; and 8 months of cash assistance from the federal Refugee Cash Assistance program (amounts vary by state and household size; Economic Services Administration, n.d.). Beyond this period, refugees may be

EXHIBIT 1.1. Refugee and Immigrant Quick Facts

- In the United States, there are an estimated 43.2 million immigrants, comprising 13.4% of the nation's population (UNHCR, 2018a, 2018b).

- There are 68.5 million forcibly displaced people worldwide (UNHCR, 2018a, 2018b).

- Of these, 25.4 million are refugees, more than half of whom are under the age of 18.

- An estimated 11.3 million immigrants in the United States (approximately one fourth) are undocumented (Zong, Batalova, & Burrows, 2019).

- The largest immigrant ethnic group in the United States is Latinx, with Mexico being the top origin country (Pew Research, 2018). Seventeen percent of Latinx children are undocumented, and approximately 40% of Latinx children have at least one parent who is undocumented (Fry & Passel, 2009).

TABLE 1.1. Definitions of Legal Statuses and Clinical Implications

Legal status	Clinical implications
Refugees	Definition: A legal status provided to individuals who are recognized by the 1951 Convention definition as persons who have crossed an international boundary because they are "unable or unwilling to avail themselves of the protection of their former country due to a well-founded fear of persecution based on race; religion; nationality; membership of a particular social group; or political opinion" (UNHCR, 1951).
	Clinical implications: Knowing the rights and benefits that refugees can claim in their state or country will allow providers to best serve these individuals. Refugees are eligible to work immediately upon arrival, and may apply for a green card one year after arrival.
Asylum seekers	Definition: Individuals who have applied for international protection but whose refugee-status claims have not been verified. Asylum seekers may have similar experiences as refugees but have not been afforded the same legal protections and benefits.
	Clinical implications: Understanding that these individuals face additional uncertainty around legal status and deportation can help providers address the unique challenges they may face.
Unaccompanied children (UAC)	Definition: Children under the age of 18 "who have been separated from both parents and other relatives and are not being cared for by an adult who, by law or custom, is responsible for doing so" (UNHCR, 1951).
	Clinical implications: A UAC's age and lack of legal status may make them particularly vulnerable to exploitation or victimization during their journey. UACs may also be accustomed to assuming adult responsibilities. A UAC may seek to remain in the country legally through applying for asylum or a Special Immigrant Juvenile Status visa. During the application process, UACs are housed under the auspices of the ORR (Office of Refugee Resettlement) in foster homes, residential centers, detention centers, or other care facilities.
Unaccompanied refugee minor (URM)	Definition: Children who enter the United States legally as refugees through the U.S. refugee admissions program, or children referred from the UAC program who have received Special Immigrant Juvenile Status. URMs typically are placed in foster care until age 21, with some benefits extending to age 23.
	Clinical implications: A URM may be placed with families whose ethnicity and associated customs differ from their own. Older children or adolescents may have functioned independently for many years and may be unaccustomed to being within a family system where they lose independence and autonomy.
Undocumented immigrant	Definition: An undocumented immigrant enters the United States without proper authorization documents or enters legally but then overstays his or her visa.
	Clinical implications: Undocumented immigrants may not access needed services out of fear that they will be reported and deported. Federal policies restrict access to federal public benefits such as food stamps and Supplemental Social Security Income (SSI), though a small number of states provide access to benefits (Fix & Passel, 2002).

eligible for several time-limited cash, medical, and social benefit programs, such as Temporary Assistance for Needy Families or Social Security, most of which benefits expire after the first five to seven years (U.S. Government Accountability Office, 2010).

The structure of these programs varies by state: Whereas the majority of programs are state-administered cash-assistance programs, a third of states operate private–public partnerships whereby cash-assistance programs are administered through local resettlement, nonprofit, or religious agencies and are integrated with case management and employment services (Office of Refugee Resettlement [ORR], 2014). The public–private partnerships provide refugees with intensive and integrated services in their first months to establish economic self-sufficiency early in resettlement, with the goal of reducing long-term dependency on welfare programs (ORR, 2014).

In contrast to refugees, asylum seekers flee from unsafe conditions in their home country to a country where they then apply for the right to remain. The circumstances that would lead someone to be considered a refugee or an asylee are fundamentally very similar; however, asylum seekers apply for protection within the country to which they have fled. The process of applying for asylum is lengthy and the outcome is uncertain. Both the legal application process and the uncertainty of its outcome can be highly stressful and retraumatizing (Procter, Kenny, Eaton, & Grech, 2018; Schock, Rosner, & Knaevelsrud, 2015). During the period when their application is under review, asylum seekers may remain in the country in which they are applying for legal status and may apply for employment authorization 150 days after filing an asylum application. While their application is pending, asylum seekers are not eligible to receive federal benefits (U.S. Citizenship and Immigration Services, 2019).

Undocumented immigrants may share many of the same experiences as refugees and asylum seekers, but they do not have legal status within the country to which they have migrated and have not applied for asylum. Within the United States, some undocumented immigrants from Central America have fled violent conflict or gang violence (or both) and desperate economic circumstances (Corsetti, 2006). Mexican and Central American immigrants make up just over half of the undocumented population within the United States (Migration Policy Institute, 2014). Undocumented immigrants face particular challenges related to discrimination, restricted access to benefits, fear of deportation, and family separations (Torres, Santiago, Walts, & Richards, 2018). Families with even one member who is not documented, or "mixed-status" families, must contend with the heightened risk and fear associated with being undocumented (Torres et al., 2018). Parental deportation can be traumatic for children in multiple ways, including by witnessing the forced removal of the parent, the sudden and unexplained absence of a parent, and the ensuing instability in housing or family functioning (Brabeck, Lykes, & Hunter, 2014).

In recent years, some countries have engaged in the practice of holding unauthorized immigrants in detention indefinitely or while asylum applications are adjudicated (Wood, 2018). Research resoundingly documents that detention has a negative impact on the mental health of asylum seekers, and in particular can be damaging to the psychological well-being of children (Fazel, Karunakara, & Newnham, 2014; Silove, Austin, & Steel, 2007). In a study of 70 detained asylum seekers, detentions were associated with significant psychological distress that worsened over the course of detention (Physicians for Human Rights & Bellevue/NYU Program for Survivors of Torture, 2003). Detention can negatively impact parents' mental health, threatening their capacity to care for their children both during and after the period of detention (Mares, 2016; Mares, Newman, Dudley, & Gale, 2002; Steel et al., 2004). Children are particularly vulnerable to the detrimental effects of detention; young children held in detention can suffer from developmental delays that impact their development long after they have left the detention center (Mares & Jureidini, 2004). In a study of 10 children ages 6 through 17 who had been referred to mental health services following a period in a detention center, 100% met criteria for both posttraumatic stress disorder and major depressive disorder with suicidal ideation (Mares & Jureidini, 2004). Detained children have also been found to have higher levels of mental health symptoms than nondetained peers (Reijneveld, de Boer, Bean, & Korfker, 2005; von Werthern et al., 2018). In Australia, where the issue of child detention has been widely debated, two inquiries found that "immigration detention has harmful health, mental health and developmental consequences for children and negative impacts on parenting" (Mares, 2016, p. 11). This conclusion is supported by research in other nations where child-detention policies have been put in place, including England (Lorek et al., 2009), Canada (Kronick, Rousseau, & Cleveland, 2011), and the Netherlands (Reijneveld et al., 2005).

In the United States, a "zero-tolerance" policy related to immigration was put in place in 2018, leading to the detention and federal prosecution of all immigrants crossing the U.S.–Mexico border without legal documentation. At the same time, a policy of family separation was implemented as, by law, children were not allowed to remain with parents who were in detention (Wood, 2018). Outcry regarding the damaging effects of family separation on child health and development eventually led to a change in the separation policy, but the practice of holding families in detention continues (Wood, 2018). Professional societies such as the American Psychological Association, the American Academy of Pediatrics, the American Medical Association, and the National Association of Social Work have strongly opposed both family separation and detention of immigrant families, declaring these practices unethical (Kraft, 2018; Madara, 2018; Mills, 2018; National Association of Social Workers, 2018).

Over the past 5 years, instability and violence in the Northern Triangle region of Central America have led to a significant increase in the migration of unaccompanied children (UAC)—that is, minors who are sent, or flee, to the United States without an adult guardian (Torres et al., 2018). According to the UNHCR, more than half of unaccompanied immigrant children are eligible for international protection (UNHCR, 2014). These children present with particular needs, both because of the lack of guardianship and because many have had to assume adult responsibilities at a young age, making it more difficult to transition into the roles expected of children within the U.S. cultural context (L. Collier, 2015). In a study comparing immigrant students who had and had not been separated from parents for extended periods, Suárez-Orozco, Bang, and Kim (2011) found that those who had been separated were more likely to report symptoms of anxiety and depression in the early years of migration. Similarly, in a study of refugee adolescents in Belgium, those who migrated without parents were more likely to have been exposed to more traumatic events and also demonstrated higher levels of mental health problems (Derluyn, Mels, & Broekaert, 2009). Thus, the stress and danger of migration in the absence of a parental figure may be particularly detrimental to the health and well-being of immigrant youth.

Common across refugees, asylum seekers, and some undocumented immigrants are the immense challenges of forced migration, the likely exposure to trauma and loss along the way, and the enormous task of acculturating to a new land and a new way of life. Despite these commonalities, however, the different legal statuses have important practical implications. Those without formal legal status may experience significant anxiety about their long-term resettlement prospects and the threat of deportation (Torres et al., 2018). Asylum seekers must go through an often arduous legal process involving detailed interviews about past trauma in order to document their necessitated departure from their country of origin. Undocumented immigrants may be afraid to seek services or turn to authorities for help and protection because of their legal status (Hacker et al., 2011). Children in mixed-status or undocumented households may be exposed to constant fear of discovery and deportation, or of separation from primary caregivers.

Additionally, neither undocumented immigrants nor asylum seekers have access to the benefits and resettlement assistance afforded to refugees. Thus, practically and clinically, legal distinctions among immigrant children and families are important to understand.

Within this book, we largely use the terms *refugee* and *immigrant* to refer to immigrants or their children who have come to the United States fleeing violence and instability in their homelands. Where particular legal statuses play a role, we more specifically reference implications for someone with refugee status, or who is an undocumented immigrant, unaccompanied child, unaccompanied refugee minor, or asylum seeker. We hope our book will be helpful for clinicians and other providers working with any child or adolescent and his or her family who is contending with acculturation and a history of trauma and loss.

One final note on terminology: Children of refugees and immigrants who are born in the United States have full citizenship but often still contend with the challenges of navigating the distinct cultures inside and outside the home, and they may also feel the effects of intergenerational trauma. Thus, much of what is described in this book will be relevant to children raised in families of refugee or immigrant origin, even if they themselves are second-generation Americans.

REFUGEE AND IMMIGRANT JOURNEYS: PREMIGRATION, MIGRATION, AND RESETTLEMENT

The journey of many refugees and immigrants can be described in several discrete phases: premigration, migration (including time spent in refugee camps or detention centers), and resettlement. Although every journey is unique, here we describe experiences typical of each phase and how this may influence working with a child or adolescent refugee or immigrant.

Premigration

Premigration refers to the period of time prior to leaving one's home country. In some countries that generate large numbers of refugees, times of relative stability are quite recent, and the premigration period may have consisted largely of peace and stability until the onset of violence. For example, prior to the outbreak of civil war in 2011, children growing up in Syria might have easily presumed they were on a path to receive a full elementary and secondary education, continue to college, and establish a career (Pearlman, 2017). Children from countries that only more recently experienced significant political and economic disruption may have strong educational backgrounds, and their parents may have obtained high levels of education (e.g., advanced degrees in medicine, law, and engineering) that may directly and indirectly aid them in navigating the resettlement process. Despite these educational and economic advantages, the relative loss of status for families who previously occupied a higher socioeconomic status— for example, one with a parent who worked as a physician and now works as a night-shift custodian—can be a major stressor and traumatic loss that can deeply affect families (Alemi, James, & Montgomery, 2016; Gans, 2009).

Some countries, in contrast, have experienced decades of upheaval and social instability. Children growing up in these contexts have never had the basic scaffolding foundational to healthy child development, such as functioning schools, clean water, safe neighborhoods, and an intact government. Refugee or immigrant children from settings of prolonged disruption may have had little or no formal education prior to resettlement, may have cognitive or health complications related to poor nutrition and sanitation, and may have lived in a state of chronic stress and adversity. Although these experiences may contribute to increased vulnerabilities that add to the challenges of resettlement, for some children and families resettlement may also offer opportunities that would never have been possible in their homelands. Girls from patriarchal cultures may see opportunities for leadership and equity (Abdi, 2014), and across families the opportunities for advancement and education may offer additional hope and motivation (Hauck, Lo, Maxwell, & Reynolds, 2014).

Clinicians will want to understand the nature of the premigration context. One key question to consider related to the premigration phase is, to what degree did the child know a life of stability and normalcy? Has the child grown up with an understanding of what a safe world looks like and, thus, can cognitively place the time of war and flight as a period of temporary disruption? Or has the child never known what it is like to be protected by laws and to be assured of food and shelter? Did early experience foster healthy development or was it beset by adversity? Understanding how a child fares in resettlement requires understanding what resources he or she had going into migration, as well as the challenges he or she currently faces. (See Exhibit 1.2.)

Migration

The decision to flee one's home country marks the beginning of the *migration* phase of the journey. For some this happens precipitously: an imminent

EXHIBIT 1.2. Key Questions About Premigration

- To what degree did the child know a life of stability and normalcy before migration?
- To what degree did the child have access to education, health care, good sanitation, security, and nutrition prior to migration?
- How long was the child exposed to adversity/instability prior to migration?
- Does the family view resettlement as holding new opportunities for themselves and their child?
- Did the caregiver experience a loss of professional status/opportunity?

threat of danger may lead to an unexpected departure with no chance to plan and gather belongings. Families may be separated. The period of flight is often exceedingly dangerous and may be marked by exhausting journeys, deprivation, chronic danger, and immense uncertainty (Lustig et al., 2004). For children who undertake this journey without their parents, whether because they flee alone as unaccompanied children or because of the separation and loss that is intrinsic to the brutality of war, their experience of migration may be one of even greater vulnerability (Derluyn et al., 2009). Remarkably, some parents are able to shield their children from the terrifying nature of the journey (Apfel & Simon, 1996). Regardless, the migration journey through which parents bring their children to safety is a testament to their strength and courage.

Immigrants crossing the border from Mexico and Central America sometimes face the double threat of both dangerous journeys and being financially beholden to violent criminal smugglers. For instance, travel by cargo train colloquially referred to as "La Bestia" is a common path for those seeking to cross into the United States via Mexico; interpersonal violence and injuries or deaths associated with falling from the train are common (Torres et al., 2018). Others suffer or die from dehydration and exposure to the elements (Fulginiti, 2008). Once in the United States, some "coyotes" (smugglers) seek to extort additional funds from families and have been known to murder people if they do not pay (Fulginiti, 2008). As noted above, others may be held in detention centers at the border, a process that may involve human-rights violations, separation from family, and uncertainty regarding deportation and family reunification (Brabeck et al., 2014). For some refugees the migration phase includes a stay in refugee camps. Refugees may live in camps for years or even decades while awaiting resettlement. Typically run by UNHCR, governments, or nongovernmental organizations (NGOs), refugee camps seek to offer shelter and food. Camps often are overcrowded, unsanitary, and dangerous (de Bruijn, 2009). Some refugee children will have spent much of their childhood in a refugee camp. Some camps offer education for children; others do not, although camp residents may informally arrange classes for children (UNHCR, 2017).

Clinicians will want to understand the nature of the migration journey. What types of trauma did the child experience on his or her journey? Was the child separated from his or her primary caregivers during this period? Was the child deprived of food, water, and other basic necessities? If yes, for how long? Was the child held in a detention facility? Is the child feeling safe and settled in his or her current social environment? Or is the child still psychologically in the migration phase, or feeling as if he or she cannot set down roots because of uncertainties in his or her current legal status? Understanding this context will help the provider address not only the child's current symptoms, but also some of the underlying drivers that might be missed without understanding the migration experience and its ongoing impact on the child. (See Exhibit 1.3.)

Resettlement

The third phase of the refugee journey is *resettlement*. Although the word *refugee* contains within it the root *refuge*, the process of resettlement can itself be fraught with stress, disappointment, and—at times—trauma. Refugees do not get to choose where they resettle and are often resettled in low-resource communities (Rawlings, Capps, Gentsch, & Fortuny, 2007; UNHCR, 2018b). As is the case in many low-resource communities, exposure to crime and neighborhood violence is not uncommon (Hecker, Fetz, Ainamani, & Elbert, 2015). Furthermore, stress and mental illness—such as posttraumatic stress disorder (PTSD), depression, and anxiety—may inhibit some refugee or immigrant parents' capacities to parent effectively (Sangalang, Jager, & Harachi, 2017). The stress of acculturation itself may tear at families and introduce conflict and loss within the home. Although initial stressors of resettlement diminish over time, the experience of acculturating to a new home and culture is an enduring experience that may lead to different

---

EXHIBIT 1.3. Key Questions About Migration

- How long was the journey (days, months, years, a generation)?
- Did the family stay in a refugee camp? If so, what camp, and what conditions?
- Did the child have access to any formal or informal education during this time?
- What kind of trauma and/or loss occurred along the way?
- Was the family separated during this time?
- Does the family have any financial obligations/demands that contribute to stress or risk?
- Is resettlement in this country legal or is the family at risk for deportation?

questions, stressors, or assets at different times in a youth's development (Collie, Kindon, Liu, & Podsiadlowski, 2010).

Overall, the process of resettlement is marked by what we call the *four core stressors*: (a) *trauma* (and the enduring emotional consequences of the adversity experienced preresettlement), (b) *resettlement stress*, (c) *acculturative stress*, and (d) *isolation.* These stressors can create significant challenges to adaptation and development, but at times can also catalyze important growth or empowerment. For instance, experiences of discrimination have been tied to higher levels of civic engagement among some immigrants (Jensen, 2010; Stepick & Stepick, 2002), and trauma can lead to positive growth (Sleijpen, Haagen, Mooren, & Kleber, 2016). Thus, although it is important to consider sources of stress and ways of mitigating them, it is equally important to recognize the strengths being brought to bear in managing such stress. Next, we briefly describe the meaning of these terms and the research that points to their importance; throughout the book the four core stressors provide a framework for understanding, assessing and treating refugee children (see Figure 1.2).

FIGURE 1.2. Refugee and Immigrant Youth Core Stressors

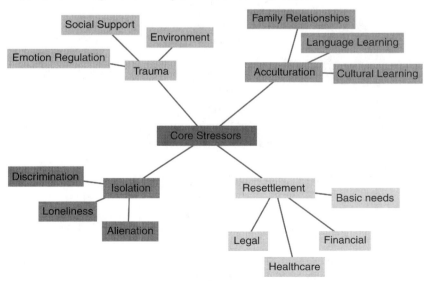

From "Refugee Services Toolkit: Model of the Four Core Stressors That Contribute to Refugee Risk and Resilience," by Refugee Trauma and Resilience Center, 2018 (http://www.childrenshospital.org/centers-and-services/programs/o-_-z/refugee-trauma-and-resilience-center-program/training-and-resource-development). Copyright 2018 by Refugee Trauma and Resilience Center. Adapted with permission.

TRAUMA, MENTAL HEALTH, AND THE RESILIENCE OF REFUGEE CHILDREN

Fundamentally, being a refugee or forcibly displaced immigrant is a socio-political phenomenon, not a personal or psychological condition. As Papadopoulos (2007) noted, "There is a tendency by mental health professionals to approach the state of being a refugee as if it were a psychological, or indeed a psychopathological, state" (p. 302). Although experiences of trauma frequently pervade multiple phases of the refugee and immigrant journey, and refugee youth do present with clinically higher prevalence rates of stress-related psychological disorders than their nonrefugee peers (Fazel & Stein, 2003), being a refugee or forcibly displaced immigrant is not synonymous with being traumatized. As is true for other populations of traumatized children (Copeland, Keeler, Angold, & Costello, 2007), even for those refugee and immigrant children who have experienced significant traumatic events, these cannot be automatically assumed to be traumatizing experiences with associated mental health problems. It is important to recognize that refugee and immigrant children—like other children who have experienced trauma—frequently show tremendous resilience despite histories of severe adversity (Keles, Friborg, Idsøe, Sirin, & Oppedal, 2018; Masten & Narayan, 2012). For instance, in a study of 918 unaccompanied refugee adolescents in Norway, the majority were determined to be either "healthy" (41.9% showed low levels of depressive symptoms at multiple time points) or "resilient" (16.4% showed decreasing levels of depressive symptoms across time; Keller, Joscelyne, Granski, & Rosenfeld, 2017). Even among refugees who do experience significant mental health symptoms, it is not unusual to see high levels of functioning as well (Kinzie, Sack, Angell, Clarke, & Ben, 1989). This broader understanding of refugee and immigrant children as diverse beings with diverse experiences and, frequently, tremendous assets, is critical to bear in mind.

Recognizing that trauma does not define the refugee experience, it is nonetheless of central importance to the treatment and recovery of some youth. Some refugee and immigrant children have experienced the worst of what humanity can be and do and must face the challenges of resettlement while also struggling with the consequences of severe trauma and related mental health problems. Rates of trauma exposure for refugee youth vary greatly depending on their country of origin and individual experiences (Benjet et al., 2016; Keller et al., 2017). Rates of mental illness similarly range widely (Dimitry, 2012; Ellis, Lincoln, et al., 2010). So although it is important to meet each new child and family with an openness to what is most important to them, for those who do experience mental illness in response to the stress and trauma of the migration experience, acknowledging and addressing past trauma may be critical to allowing them to move beyond it.

BEYOND THE TRAUMA LENS: RESETTLEMENT, ACCULTURATION, AND ISOLATION

Although trauma, both past and present, can be a significant factor in a refugee or immigrant child's adjustment, these experiences need to be understood in the context of other stressors that fundamentally shape the resettlement experience: resettlement, acculturation, and isolation. Children's social environments (e.g., family context, school, neighborhood, broader community) can be a source of strength and positivity for youth who are coping with psychological distress (Torres et al., 2018); however, these social ecosystems can also generate stress that impedes recovery (Porter & Haslam, 2005). It is essential, therefore, to assess the social environment and, if indicated, directly address environmental stressors as one component of treatment. social environment

Resettlement stress refers to the challenges associated with accessing basic resources and services that families need, such as financial stability and health care. Although stress related to meeting these needs is not unique to refugees, accessing critical resources can be especially difficult for refugee families in a new and unfamiliar system. In particular, immigrant and refugee families may struggle to attain proper health care, legal assistance, financial stability, and basic resources such as clothing, housing, and food. Resettlement stress is associated with higher symptoms of posttraumatic stress disorder in refugees (Perera et al., 2013). For newly arrived families, immediate distress related to basic needs like food and shelter can often and understandably overshadow concerns about mental health. Providers can build trust and increase engagement with refugee and immigrant families by acknowledging and assisting with resettlement stressors. Subsequent chapters in this volume provide guidance on assessing (Chapter 4) and managing (Chapter 5) resettlement stressors in treatment.

Acculturative stress refers to the challenges inherent to adjusting to a new culture and language. These challenges include language fluency and the benefits associated with being fluent in a country's dominant language; comfort and fluency in the local language often unlock multiple pathways to economic and social opportunities in a new country. Even a decade after resettlement, higher language fluency is associated with greater odds of employment and lower symptoms of psychological distress (Beiser & Hou, 2001). The acculturation process unfolds differently for newcomers based on a multitude of factors including age, socioeconomic status (SES), and country of origin. Members of the same family may adjust at different rates, with children learning the new language more quickly and more readily adopting cultural norms (Chudek, Cheung, & Heine, 2015). This can cause strain within families if children are perceived as too "Americanized" by the older generation or lose a common language with their family.

Families may also experience the fourth core stressor, *isolation stress*, as a result of discrimination, alienation, and loneliness. Social support and feelings of belonging can greatly bolster mental health, even in the face of extreme adversity, whereas isolation is recognized as a primary risk factor for psychological distress and early mortality (Holt-Lunstad, Smith, Baker, Harris, & Stephenson, 2015). Reestablishing supportive social networks and fostering broader community narratives of belonging and acceptance can help children and families feel as though they belong in their new home.

Visible minority refugees and immigrants in the United States (e.g., people of color, Muslim youth who wear a hijab) may be especially vulnerable to experiences of discrimination and, consequently, poor mental health outcomes (Ellis, MacDonald, et al., 2010; Hadley & Patil, 2009). Many refugee youths occupy multiple historically marginalized social and cultural identities, and it is the dynamic interaction of these and other identities that form what these youths experience and how they are treated in their new home (e.g., Ellis, Lincoln, et al., 2018; Roxas & Roy, 2012). In Chapter 2, we examine how *intersectionality* (i.e., the interconnected nature of social-identity categorization) may be an especially effective framework when working with refugee youth.

Throughout this book, we use the framework of the four core stressors to understand common refugee and immigrant experiences and to inform effective clinical practice and intervention. This includes recognizing gaps of service and support in the social environment that can be directly addressed in treatment, as well as building on the individual and community strengths that refugee and immigrant youth and families demonstrate. Chapter 4 guides the reader through the process of assessing the family's strengths and needs according to the four core stressors and integrating your findings into treatment planning. Chapters 5 and 6 suggest strategies and interventions to address these stressors in the social environment.

In summary, we introduced several organizing frameworks for conceptualizing the experiences and needs of refugees and immigrants. Formal legal categories divide immigrants into multiple categories including refugees, asylum seekers, unaccompanied children and undocumented immigrants—each associated with different levels of vulnerability and assistance in resettlement settings. We explored some of the common challenges and risks refugees and immigrants face across the three phases of refugee migration journeys: premigration, migration, and resettlement. Finally, we pointed to the four core stressors of trauma, resettlement, acculturation, and isolation that can exacerbate psychological distress upon resettlement. Each of these frameworks helps to guide a clinician's understanding of how the political and social environment shapes a refugee or immigrant child's present functioning, and how intervention can best support a youth's positive adaptation.

2 WORKING CROSS-CULTURALLY

difficulties connecting w/ parents from dif cultures

A young psychologist was working at a school with a large number of immigrant and refugee children. She recognized that some of the children were displaying emotional and behavioral concerns, but she had been unable to gain consent from the parents for mental health services for their children. She decided to run a group for parents of refugee and immigrant backgrounds to help provide skills for adjusting to life in the United States, with the additional hope of increasing the likelihood that parents would consent to mental health services.

After the first group meeting, she sought help from her supervisor regarding how to handle parents' discussions of cultural practices around mental health. She gave an example of a Latina mother who talked about her son having experienced *susto* (a fright) during their migration. The son was now often sad and self-isolating. The mother had explained that in her culture this was cured by a *curandero* (a healer) and had asked if the psychologist could help her locate such a healer. The young psychologist also spoke about a mother from the Middle East who told her that her son was brilliant as a younger boy, and people used to admire and talk about him. The mother had then explained that this had led to an "evil eye" striking him. For this she was seeking a *sheikh* (a religious healer) who could read the Koran over him to exorcise the evil. Finally, she described a mother from East Africa who had

she wants a healer, not meds

http://dx.doi.org/10.1037/0000163-002
Mental Health Practice With Immigrant and Refugee Youth: A Socioecological Framework,
by B. H. Ellis, S. M. Abdi, and J. P. Winer

said that her daughter woke up screaming at night, did not eat, and was often angry. The mother said she had seen this before and that it was caused by *jinn*, or possession by spirits. After describing what had transpired in the group, the psychologist despairingly asked her supervisor, "How do I offer my clinical services when these parents seem to have a different understanding of what the problem is and how to treat it?"

As we can see in the opening vignette, providers working with refugee and immigrant communities must often navigate cultural practices and beliefs that inform the client's and family's understanding of the issues that brought them to the provider. In this chapter, we discuss some of the challenges that working cross-culturally poses for providers. We then share three core strategies for reducing these challenges: (a) enhancing cultural competence, (b) taking a stance of cultural humility, and (c) working with cultural brokers.

[handwritten: ways to navigate dif cultural practices]

STRATEGIES FOR PROVIDING CULTURALLY RESPONSIVE MENTAL HEALTH CARE

Within refugee communities of historically collectivist cultural backgrounds, the experience of psychological illness is often attributed to culture-specific or religious phenomena or to both. In many cultures, illness may not be conceived as situated in either the body or mind alone but may be seen as drawing on physical, supernatural, and moral realms. Mental illness may be understood as influenced by ancestors and spirits rather than internal emotional factors. The notion that "traumatic stress" causes psychological disruption may be invalid in a society that emphasizes fate, determinism, and spiritual influences (Chan, Ying Ho, & Chow, 2002). For example, within Nepali–Bhutanese communities, mental illness might be attributed to *karma* or a curse in the family dynasty, and help might be sought from a traditional healer (i.e., a *dhami*). In Somali culture, impairing psychological symptoms might be attributed to possession by spirits, and a religious leader (i.e., a *sheikh* or *wadaad*) with special skills in exorcising spirits might be seen as the appropriate authority to treat this type of problem. For many people of Central American and Latin American backgrounds, an indigenous healing method that may be sought for emotional distress is *curanderismo*, which involves a number of treatments, including "herbal remedies, breathing exercises, sweating, massage, incantations, and ritual cleansing treatments" (Falicov, 2014, p. 207). Psychological suffering that might commonly fall under the auspices of a psychologist, social worker, or psychiatrist in Western countries might be seen by some refugee and immigrant populations as having an etiology and treatment that have nothing to do with mental health service providers.

Refugee and immigrant communities bring with them perspectives and understandings about the development, maintenance, and treatment of psychological suffering that may be different than those of the providers and systems they interface with in resettlement. Given these diverse perspectives, a shared understanding between providers and families of how families conceptualize the cause and proposed treatment of an observable problem is crucial for establishing effective collaboration, trust, and healing. The goal is not to convince a client or family that the historically Western model is "correct"; rather, the goal is to acknowledge and validate that there are many truths and that joining together is the most effective way to build a path toward healing. One of the initial and most common barriers to effective treatment for refugee and immigrant youth is that the family and the clinician are not aligned with regard to the identified problem, the identified treatment process, and the explanation(s) as to why and how this treatment may be a wise choice of action. If the treatment alliance is ruptured within the first encounters, it is unlikely that families will stay engaged in services. Below is an example of how a well-intentioned but ineffective clinical interaction regarding a 15-year-old Somali refugee boy presenting with disruptive behavior issues might unfold. The vignette demonstrates how, even as the clinician attempts to come to a common understanding of the issue, the clinician and caregiver become less and less aligned.

CLINICIAN: [*after gathering information from multiple sources with the aid of an interpreter*] Ms. Hassan, your child has what we call PTSD, because of what happened during the war. The trauma your child experienced can leave lasting impacts on how he feels and how he acts. This can make it difficult for him to do well in school. It can also cause him to struggle with relationships both at home and at school. He might be easily startled, might feel anxious and fearful in class, and might be so symptomatic that he cannot focus on studies. This also might be the reason your child is getting into fights in school and at home. I am looking forward to helping you.

PARENT: No, my child was only 5 years old when the war happened. How can the war impact him? I have gone through the war, and I am able to wake up every morning and go to work

parent may not understand

and take care of my family. The problem is that my child has changed. He is no longer a child who respects his parents. He is not a good child. He is doing things that are against our cultural beliefs, and that is the reason he is getting in trouble. You need to teach this child to be a good child. He needs to hear from you that the things he is doing are not good. That he needs to change. In our culture it is the job of the adults to criticize and discipline children when they don't do what is expected of them. Here in America, adults are not doing a good job of telling the kids to be good. In school, my son is not punished when he breaks the rules. How is he going to learn that he needs to change his behavior if adults are not showing their disappointment in him?

CLINICIAN: Your child is suffering from PTSD because of what happened in the war. His behavior is out of his control. He needs help and support to recover—he doesn't need punishment. In addition to psychotherapy, he may benefit from a medication to help him with his symptoms. I am happy to provide a referral to a child psychiatrist.

PARENT: Medication?! No, no, my child does not need medication. He is not crazy. I have seen this medication and what it does to children. Once they have taken those pills they never return to normal. This child just needs to be good. He needs to change. He needs *dhaqan celis* (return to his culture). I will send him back to Somalia so that he can be taught how to behave. This happens to our children when they lose our culture and they become too Americanized. They lose respect for their elders and they become lazy. Children need strict physical discipline and rules. In America they do whatever they want!

[handwritten margin note: very against medication]

After some continued ineffective back and forth, the session ends abruptly and the mother leaves the office.

Later that day, because of significant ethical concerns that the child is not getting the care he needs and that his mother is threatening a dangerous action of physical harm as well as sending him back to an active war zone, the clinician determines he must report the family to child protection services. The clinician, with the aid of a phone interpreter, calls the mother the next day to let her know he was mandated to file a child protection report regarding possible neglect and abuse.

PARENT: What? You are saying I neglect and abuse my child? I brought him from war. I sacrificed everything in my life to bring him here. Now you, who I've only just met, are telling me how to parent and that my son would be better off with strangers?! This is my nightmare! People in power telling us how to live! I thought we left our bad times behind us.

In spite of the clinician's best intentions, the above encounter likely causes more harm than good. Here the parent and clinician are operating under very different cultural scripts. The clinician, armed with his knowledge of trauma and its potential negative effects on the psychological well-being of children, seeks to provide the best care but does not have the cultural skills to effectively engage the parent in services. Although well-intentioned and well-versed in scientific understandings of trauma, the clinician lacked cultural attunement and understanding of how the parent was making meaning of the problem. Evidence-based practice calls for the thoughtful integration of scientific evidence, clinician expertise, and patient values and preference, with cultural context informing each aspect and delivery of these components (American Psychological Association [APA] Presidential Task Force on Evidence-Based Practice, 2006). As is clear, this encounter decreases the likelihood that this mother will engage her child in treatment with this clinician, and also likely decreases the chances that she will seek psychological services for him again.

Refugees and immigrants come to services with their own understanding of what emotional suffering looks like, when and where to go for help, and what healing looks like. Providers also come to their work with culturally bound ways of seeing what emotional suffering looks like, when and where someone should go for help, and what healing looks like. This understanding is shaped by their own culture and identities, as well as by their disciplinary training and practice. The sooner providers acknowledge that, like the diverse clients they hope to serve, they too are cultural beings, the sooner they will be able to provide more effective and responsive services. What follows are three strategies for enhancing culturally responsive practice with refugee and immigrant communities: (a) enhancing cultural competency, (b) taking a stance of cultural humility, and (c) working with cultural brokers.

Cultural Competence

The National Child Traumatic Stress Network has defined *cultural competence* as "the capacity of programs to provide services in ways that are acceptable, engaging and effective with multicultural populations" (Birman et al., 2005,

p. 12). As defined by Sue and Sue (2017), cultural competence is "the awareness, knowledge, and skills needed to function effectively with culturally diverse populations" (p. 747). Cultural competence can be enhanced at various levels of the health care and social services ecosystem, from the individual through the institutional. One way in which systems have attempted to enhance providers' ability to provide culturally responsive care is through the provision of cultural competency training (e.g., Betancourt, Green, Carrillo, & Ananeh-Firempong, 2003; Butler et al., 2011; Gregg & Saha, 2006). As discussed further below, although cultural competency as a framework has great value to add, this type of training and knowledge development must be approached as more than just learning facts about a cultural group.

At times, cultural competence is narrowly understood in organizations as prescriptive things to say and do and things to not say and do when working with specific social and cultural groups. Certain competency strategies or principles may be transcultural, meaning they may be important to employ across all populations, whereas other strategies or principles may be specific to a cultural group. For instance, whereas the principles of trust and respect generally are considered universal, the specific strategies for how to greet someone in a way that communicates respect and builds trust varies from culture to culture. Common strategies for increasing cultural competency in service systems often include providing training and workshops to learn specific information to enhance clinical encounters (APA, 2017). For example, if a provider is meeting with a Muslim person of a different gender, it is culturally appropriate to wait for the client to initiate a handshake. Additionally, increasing the availability and accessibility of interpreters or translators may also greatly enhance cultural competence through enhanced patient-provider communication, assessment, and treatment delivery.

Across all these examples, and related systems-based cultural competency interventions, the pedagogical assumption is that the more an individual or system learns about another culture, the more effective and knowledgeable they will be when engaging with that culture. The strengths of a cultural competency approach are that it may increase the foundational knowledge that systems or individuals have about specific groups and may reduce the perpetration of overt culturally insensitive practices. The limitations of a cultural competency approach include unintentionally stereotyping groups by taking one "truth" and applying it too broadly, ignoring or undervaluing diversities within social and cultural groups, or superficially adapting interventions in ways that add no new value or even create aversive bias by making providers believe they are being culturally responsive (e.g., Kirmayer, 2012).

The cultural competency approach has been critiqued for perpetuating ideas that cultures are monolithic and for unintentionally ignoring diversity within cultural and linguistic groups (DelVecchio Good & Hannah, 2015). Furthermore, the notion that one can learn and gain competency of an entire culture can create a false sense of expertise, when what is additionally needed is awareness, self-reflection, and thoughtful attention to each person's unique needs, circumstances, and broader context. A narrow focus on learning facts about specific cultures can also blind us to the intersectionality that informs all of our thoughts, feelings, and behaviors. *Intersectionality* refers to the way in which we are all the product of multiple, interacting social and cultural identities (APA, 2017). Some of these identities may be historically or currently privileged or culturally dominant, and some may be historically or currently marginalized or oppressed. Youth and families of refugee and immigrant backgrounds often occupy multiple historically marginalized social and cultural identities and are often confronted with new or changing identities ascribed to them across migration and resettlement. For instance, a refugee from Rwanda may experience intersecting identities of Rwandan, Christian, and immigrant; within the United States the same individual may become aware of his racial identity and be seen or labeled by others as a "person of color." Given the vast complexity and changing nature of culture and identity, taking a stance of cultural humility can enhance providers' abilities to more effectively serve diverse populations, as well as better understand ways that one's *own* identity shapes each encounter.

Cultural Humility

Whereas the framework of cultural competency focuses on learning about an individual client's culture, the framework of cultural humility encourages and empowers providers to thoughtfully interrogate their *own* culture and identities, and how these identities interact with other people's identities as well as broader sociocultural systems. In doing so, cultural humility seeks to address deficiencies, biases, and oppressive practices that contribute to health disparities. One analogy for considering the similarities and differences in the cultural competency and cultural humility pedagogies is that cultural competency may be more akin to crystallized intelligence, or learning that is concrete and fact-based, whereas cultural humility may be more akin to fluid intelligence, which includes emotional attunement, psychological flexibility, and novel problem-solving (Cattell, 1963). Both are important, and often are most effective when used collaboratively.

In formulating the initial concept of cultural humility, Tervalon and Murray-García (1998) argued that culturally responsive systems of care need to promote provider commitment to lifelong learning, self-awareness, self-reflection, and self-critique. A commitment to cultural humility calls for developing mutually beneficial and nonpaternalistic relationships between providers and communities. Cultural humility does not call for abandoning commitment to learning about specific cultures but rather aims to cultivate a corresponding focus on providers' own identities, biases, and cultural blind spots, as well as the unequal and often oppressive relationship that providers have with the historically marginalized and invalidated communities they aim to serve (Foronda, Baptiste, Reinholdt, & Ousman, 2016). Taking a culturally humble stance encourages individuals to ask not only clients to change, learn, and grow in order to heal, but for providers to do the same (Chang, Simon, & Dong, 2012). It is through the combination of learning about those we serve as well as learning about ourselves that we can achieve more effective and accessible mental health services for refugee and immigrant communities.

Bridging Cultural and Linguistic Barriers

The integration of strategies of cultural competence (e.g., culture-specific knowledge) and cultural humility (e.g., a curious, thoughtful, and culture-focused self-reflective stance) will likely foster the most culturally responsive practices. Yet, even with these two approaches, challenges remain to overcoming cultural and linguistic barriers. Bilingual providers and thoughtful use of interpreters can help overcome these barriers. A third strategy—partnering with cultural brokers—provides a particularly powerful model for providing culturally responsive care.

As defined by Jezewski (1990), *cultural brokering* is "the act of bridging, linking, or mediating between groups or persons of different cultural backgrounds for the purpose of reducing conflict or producing change" (p. 497). In some mental health care settings cultural brokers partner with clinicians to provide linguistic and cultural interpretation and to facilitate bidirectional transference of knowledge between patients and providers. Cultural brokers are distinct from interpreters in that, in addition to being fluent in both languages spoken in the intervention room, they are also dyadic partners in the content of clinical encounters. This means that they are encouraged to provide, when indicated, culturally specific information to enhance the exchange of ideas and information between the clinician and the client (Hook, 2014; Raval, 2005; Singh, McKay, & Singh, 1999). Cultural brokers

[handwritten margin note: Someone to help connect the two cultures]

speak the same language and are often members of the same ethnocultural community as the refugee and immigrant families an organization hopes to serve, and they may also have had direct experience as refugees or immigrants themselves. Cultural brokers should ideally possess knowledge of mental illness and psychological suffering as conceived by the cultural group of the individual(s) seeking services, and of the broader cultural context in which they are situated (Singh et al., 1999).

In some health care settings, case managers, community health workers, and patient navigators may be existing job descriptions that could be used as mechanisms to integrate cultural brokers into service delivery (Witmer, Seifer, Finocchio, Leslie, & O'Neil, 1995). *Community health workers* (CHWs) are defined as "community members who work almost exclusively in community settings and who serve as connectors between health care consumers and providers to promote health among groups that have traditionally lacked access to adequate care" (Witmer et al., 1995, p. 1055). *Patient navigators* are similar to CHWs in that they work to enhance access to health care for specific communities. Patient navigators work inside the system to address barriers that contribute to health disparities, such as lack of insurance and lack of access to transportation, or lack of knowledge of care systems among historically underserved communities (Dohan & Schrag, 2005). The role of *cultural broker* may expand beyond those of a case manager, CHW, and patient navigator, but these more commonly funded positions can provide a foundation for beginning to integrate cultural brokers into systems of care. For instance, a program in Lewiston, Maine, hired cultural brokers through the state's case management program. In addition to engaging in the dyadic work inherent to the cultural broker–clinician partnership, this case management program has provided cultural brokers with a formal mechanism through which they can work closely with clients outside of session to address core stressors negatively affecting the family system (Behrens, 2017).

Although cultural brokers may provide interpretation, they are unlike traditional interpreters in that they are integral members of a treatment dyad. The clinician–cultural broker dyads ideally meet both before and after a session to anticipate and debrief potential cultural perspectives that may influence treatment. During the session itself, the cultural broker, who holds a deep understanding of both the culture of mental health treatment as well as the culture of the client, can facilitate additional communication between clinician and client when he or she observes a gap in understanding. The addition of cultural brokers into the clinical session transforms a dyadic relationship between the clinicians and the client into a therapeutic triad; this can pose challenges for all parties. As a result, the addition of cultural brokers into therapeutic relationships should be done thoughtfully with rigorous training and supervision of both clinicians and cultural brokers. Furthermore, there are specific competencies, such as the capacity to respect confidentiality and ensure the security of protected health information, and adherence to other ethical standards that cultural brokers must possess in order to be effective in this role (National Center for Cultural Competence, Georgetown University Center for Child and Human Development, & Georgetown University Medical Center, 2007).

If a cultural broker is not available to support clinical work, interpreters may be used. Interpreters differ from cultural brokers in that they are mandated to interpret word-for-word what is said and are not at liberty to summarize or contextualize information. Interpretation in service-delivery settings can occur in person or through phone or video technology. If an ethnic community is particularly small or tightly knit, phone interpretation may be preferable because it affords more confidentiality. For in-person sessions, partnering with a professional interpreter who can attend sessions consistently may greatly strengthen the working alliance between all participants (Raval & Tribe, 2014). Best practices for a clinical session inclusive of a clinician, interpreter, and client include organizing the physical clinical space as a therapeutic triad where all parties can make eye contact and physically communicate that each member is a valued participant in the interaction (Hetherington, 2012; Hunt & Swartz, 2017; Miller, Martell, Pazdirek, Caruth, & Lopez, 2005; Tribe & Lane, 2009). Although interpreters may speak the same language (e.g., Spanish) as a client, they may be from a different cultural background (e.g., Spain vs. Colombia), and therefore aspects of meaning may be missed even when they are technically speaking the same language; for this reason, *cultural congruence* between interpreter and client is preferred if possible.

INTEGRATING CULTURALLY RESPONSIVE PRACTICES INTO CLINICAL ENCOUNTERS

Recall the clinical encounter at the beginning of the chapter that ended in a frustrated therapist and an angry, disillusioned mother. How might cultural competency and cultural humility training have shaped the encounter differently?

An alternative approach that the clinician could have taken is to prepare for the session by learning about Somali perspectives on mental illness before the encounter. The clinician might have read that Somali parents perceive certain mental health–related behaviors as *assiwalidiin*, or being disrespectful to parents and elders (Betancourt, Frounfelker, Mishra, Hussein, & Falzarano, 2015). He might have further read that in the Somali collectivist culture, all adults are expected to reinforce community norms: Parents often bring children to providers expecting that the providers will join them in disciplining the child so that they are no longer disrespectful to their elders. Equipped with this knowledge, and adopting a stance of cultural humility, the clinician might have started the session by asking the mother questions about her understanding of her child's symptoms, thereby gaining knowledge about her particular perspective and about how these symptoms are both understood and addressed in her culture. In addition, the clinician might have learned prior to the session that the term *PTSD* does not have meaning in Somali culture, and that concrete language around a child's observable behaviors would ensure that both clinician and client were talking about the same set of problems. Finally, he could have been more aware of the stigma attached to psychopharmacology and might have chosen not to raise this treatment suggestion in the first session. By approaching the meeting with competency and humility, the clinician could have more effectively created a safe space for the parent to express her fears and to hear the clinician's recommendations even if they were not aligned with what she would have done in her Somali culture.

If the provider had access to the support of a cultural broker, the cultural broker could have acted as a bridge between the clinician and the mother in multiple ways. In the presession meeting, the cultural broker could have provided the clinician with the above information about assiwalidiin. The cultural broker could then have helped the clinician think of language that would help provide and establish a common goal and understanding between the clinician and the mother. During the session, the cultural broker might have shared additional information with the clinician about how sending a child back home to Somalia is seen as a way to help save them (not neglect or child endangerment) and that although frequently mentioned in the community it was infrequently done, thus reducing the likelihood that the clinician would see this as a child-protection issue. The cultural broker might also have explained to the mother that mental health providers do not provide punishment for children when they misbehave but, nonetheless, have strategies that often help to reduce the misbehavior. In sum, a cultural broker could have acted as a bridge between the clinician and patient, acting as an interpreter not just of words, but also of experiences and cultural markers that could have helped the provider to better understand the patient, and the patient to better understand and trust the provider. Further strategies and examples of culturally responsive thinking are provided in the Table 2.1.

TABLE 2.1. A Guide to Culturally Responsive Thinking in a Clinical Encounter

Clinical issue to be addressed	Questions to ask the caregiver	Pay attention to	Additional prompts	Example of culturally responsive framing
Determine the patient's understanding of the visit.	What brought you here today? Who identified the issue that is being addressed in the intervention?	Whether the problem is identified by the parent or others, such as school personnel, and whether the parent's explanation aligns with what is on the referral.	What would be different if this was happening in their country of origin? Would this still be seen as a problem? Would the parent or child have sought outside help with this issue in their country of origin? What words or terms would have been used to describe this type of a problem or situation in the home country?	"I want to make sure that you and I have a common understanding of the problem and what we can do to make things better. You know your child better than anyone, so I need your help to understand what your child needs and how I can help."
Establish the caregiver's expectations for seeking care for the child and the outcome they are hoping to attain.	What would you like to see change in the issues that brought you here today? How can I support you in achieving the goals that you have for your child?	The client's identified source of pain and their hoped-for goals.	"Tell me what you think I can do to help you achieve this? Who else can support you in this?"	"I know that you love your child and you have worked so hard to bring your child to safety. I know that your child's education is important to you. I am here to support your child achieve his or her goals."

Assess the family's understanding of the cause of these symptoms.	What do you think is the reason your child is having these problems?	Whether parent attributes the issue to child's individual failings, religious or spiritual explanation, other culturally bound explanations.	"How is this child different from other children? How would you address these issues back home in your country of origin? Who would help you with these problems? What do you think will make this better?"	"There can be multiple causes for this problem. This is why we need to try different things to try to make it better."
Determine who the family usually goes to for help for these types of issues, and who else is involved in decision making around the child's care.	Who else have you sought help from (or do you plan to seek help from)? What do these "helpers" do? What do they think about your being here? How do these helpers understand what is going on?	Whether patient is able to identify Western-style health care interventions as an option; whether the family is engaging traditional healing mechanisms.	Have you been able to seek help from these identified helpers? What has been the outcome? Is the intervention provided by these individuals still going on? How do you see my work and these traditional helpers' roles interfacing or working together?	"I see that you are doing everything possible to help your child. Different cultures have different ways of dealing with this. As long as it is not harmful to your child, I am not asking you to stop what your culture has always done. I would love to understand it and learn from it."
Determine the family's past experience with health and social services systems.	What has your experience been with other providers in your country of origin? What about in this country?	If the patient had negative experiences, find out why and take these past experiences into account.	What was helpful? What was not? What did you wish they did differently?	"I know that sometimes in these systems parents feel helpless and lost. I want you to know that I will work with you to support your child and we will move forward only when you are ready to move forward."

Providing culturally responsive and linguistically accessible mental health services opens the door for refugees and immigrants to heal from psychological distress and to build healthy and productive lives of purpose in their new communities. For further reading on putting principles of multicultural psychology into practice, see the APA's (2017) *Multicultural Guidelines: An Ecological Approach to Context, Identity, and Intersectionality*. Their comprehensive list of 10 multicultural guidelines for psychologists and other health care providers is included as Exhibit 2.1.

Training organizations and providers to use the skills outlined through the pedagogies of both cultural competency and cultural humility increases the likelihood of improved and sustainable services (Horvat, Horey, Romios, & Kis-Rigo, 2014; Thackrah & Thompson, 2013). Cultural competency, cultural humility, and—when possible—partnering with cultural brokers not only can help with individual clinical encounters but also can enrich and shape the entire system of care, as well as that system of care's relationship with refugee and immigrant communities.

EXHIBIT 2.1. American Psychological Association's *Multicultural Guidelines: An Ecological Approach to Context, Identity, and Intersectionality*, 2017

1. Psychologists seek to recognize and understand that identity and self-definition are fluid and complex and that the interaction between the two is dynamic. To this end, psychologists appreciate that intersectionality is shaped by the multiplicity of the individual's social contexts.

2. Psychologists aspire to recognize and understand that, as cultural beings, they hold attitudes and beliefs that can influence their perceptions of and interactions with others, as well as their clinical and empirical conceptualizations. As such, psychologists strive to move beyond conceptualizations rooted in categorical assumptions, biases, and/or formulations based on limited knowledge about individuals and communities.

3. Psychologists strive to recognize and understand the role of language and communication through engagement that is sensitive to the lived experience of the individual, couple, family, group, community, and/or organizations with whom they interact. Psychologists also seek to understand how they bring their own language and communication to these interactions.

4. Psychologists endeavor to be aware of the role of the social and physical environment in the lives of clients, students, research participants, and/or consultees.

5. Psychologists aspire to recognize and understand historical and contemporary experiences with power, privilege, and oppression. As such, they seek to address institutional barriers and related inequities, disproportionalities, and disparities of law enforcement, administration of criminal justice, education, mental health, and other systems as they seek to promote justice, human rights, and access to quality and equitable mental and behavioral health services.

EXHIBIT 2.1. American Psychological Association's *Multicultural Guidelines: An Ecological Approach to Context, Identity, and Intersectionality,* 2017 (*Continued*)

6. Psychologists seek to promote culturally adaptive interventions and advocacy within and across systems, including prevention, early intervention, and recovery.

7. Psychologists endeavor to examine the profession's assumptions and practices within an international context, whether domestically or internationally based, and consider how this globalization has an impact on the psychologist's self-definition, purpose, role, and function.

8. Psychologists seek awareness and understanding of how developmental stages and life transitions intersect with the larger biosociocultural context, how identity evolves as a function of such intersections, and how these different socialization and maturation experiences influence worldview and identity.

9. Psychologists strive to conduct culturally appropriate and informed research, teaching, supervision, consultation, assessment, interpretation, diagnosis, dissemination, and evaluation of efficacy as they address the first four levels of the Layered Ecological Model of the Multicultural Guidelines.

10. Psychologists actively strive to take a strength-based approach when working with individuals, families, groups, communities, and organizations that seeks to build resilience and decrease trauma within the sociocultural context.

LIST OF RESOURCES

Tools for enhancing cultural self-awareness:

- Hays, P. A. (2016). *Addressing cultural complexities in practice: Assessment, diagnosis, and therapy* (3rd ed.). Washington, DC: American Psychological Association.
- Project Implicit (https://implicit.harvard.edu/implicit/).
- http://www.Multiculturalpsychology.com
- Cultural brokering resources (https://nccc.georgetown.edu/culturalbroker/).

3 ENGAGING REFUGEE AND IMMIGRANT FAMILIES IN MENTAL HEALTH SERVICES

A 9-year-old Somali boy and his mother, having arrived early to their appointment at the local hospital's child psychiatry clinic, are in the waiting room. A clinician calls them into the office when the hospital interpreter arrives and begins to explain the process of consent and confidentiality. Before the interpreter has a chance to interpret this for the mother, the mother hands a piece of paper to the interpreter and speaks at length in her native language. The interpreter turns back to the clinician with a somewhat sheepish look on his face and says, "She says her son isn't crazy and doesn't need to see you. She would like you to sign this paper so that he can go back to school; the school says he can't return until you do so." The paper in front of the clinician asks for verification that she has fully assessed the boy for mental health problems and that he is safe to return to school.

The central theme of the vignette above plays out in many different ways, in many different mental health offices. For some refugee families, mental health services are seen as useless at best, damaging and toxic to their family and community at worst. A common impetus for attending a mental health appointment is a mandated referral by a school that is struggling to understand and manage a refugee youth's disruptive behavior in the classroom.

http://dx.doi.org/10.1037/0000163-003

Mental Health Practice With Immigrant and Refugee Youth: A Socioecological Framework, by B. H. Ellis, S. M. Abdi, and J. P. Winer

More frequently, however, a child and parent never even make it to the office. Refugee children are grossly underserved by the current mental health system (Betancourt et al., 2017). In a study of Somali refugee adolescents in New England, only 8% of those who met full criteria for PTSD had ever sought or received any kind of mental health services (Ellis, Lincoln, et al., 2010). Understanding the barriers to mental health care is critical for developing effective and sustainable strategies to overcome them. In this chapter, we review four key barriers to engaging refugee and immigrant communities in mental health services, and corresponding strategies to address these barriers to engagement. The four key barriers are primacy of resettlement stress, distrust of authority and power, stigma of mental illness, and language and cultural barriers. Each of these barriers needs to be attended to in order to facilitate refugee children and youth's access to mental health services. Depending on the family's and the community's needs, a provider or a system of care might need to identify and address additional barriers as well.

BARRIER 1: PRIMACY OF RESETTLEMENT STRESSORS

Over the first few years of resettlement, refugees need to manage a tremendous number of challenges. Ensuring that their families have sufficient food and safe housing, can procure employment, are learning or improving their knowledge of the predominant language, and are simply navigating the day-to-day realities of a new culture may both be consuming and take priority over other tasks (Betancourt, Abdi, et al., 2015). Spending time meeting with a mental health provider who does not offer direct, concrete support around these basic needs may be seen as a waste of time. Relatedly, spending time on the emotional or behavioral needs of one child within a large family may be hard to justify when that time could be spent seeking resources to meet the basic needs of the entire family. Research suggests that, in fact, resettlement stressors significantly contribute to mental health problems and are themselves important mental health–related treatment targets (Alemi et al., 2016; Ryan, Dooley, & Benson, 2008; Teodorescu, Heir, Hauff, Wentzel-Larsen, & Lien, 2012).

Mental health providers who narrowly define the scope of treatment and expect refugee families to fully and independently find help for resettlement stress elsewhere miss important opportunities for engagement, establishing trust, and, ultimately, effective treatment. This does not mean that mental health providers who are less well versed in social service systems need to change the scope of their practice, but it does mean they need to be willing actively to engage clients and allied professionals with greater knowledge of local and national services in connecting the dots for the families they serve. A therapist could spend 6 months trying to motivate a family to investigate local transportation options in order to make trips to the grocery store easier, but a thoughtful 15-minute call with the family in the office to a local transportation agency to engage a free and safe-rides program may have greater impact.

Sometimes a child's mental health problems may contribute to or exacerbate resettlement stress. For instance, a parent who repeatedly is asked to pick up a child from school because of behavioral problems may have difficulty keeping a job. Recognizing the impact that a child's mental illness has on resettlement stressors and providing hope to families that this may change through treatment may also increase engagement. Failure to account for the barrier posed by the primacy of resettlement stressors in the lives of refugees can lead to a dissonance between what the provider thinks is important for the family's well-being and what the family feels is important. In turn, this can contribute to families rejecting mental health services. Exhibit 3.1 introduces approaches to addressing resettlement stressors, such as providing a bridge to other service providers, providing integrated care, and framing resettlement stressors as central components of the treatment plan. Chapter 5 provides more detail on how to address resettlement stressors as part of treatment.

BARRIER 2: DISTRUST OF AUTHORITY AND POWER

Lack of trust is a key barrier to mental health access for refugees and immigrants (Colucci, Minas, Szwarc, Guerra, & Paxton, 2015). Power differentials inherent in the therapist–client relationship contribute to this. Health care providers typically have more social and economic power than refugee and immigrant clients and have a better understanding of the rules and regulations of the community that they now both occupy. Furthermore, mental health providers have access to critical knowledge, resources, and social capital that are beyond the reach of many of the refugees and immigrants they seek to help. They also hold the power and mandate to report suspected child abuse and neglect to social services. As a result, they may be seen as agents of the government.

It is quite understandable that many refugees often distrust authority figures and those in power. Refugees have often experienced horrific abuse

EXHIBIT 3.1. Primacy of Resettlement Stressors

Resettlement stressors in the clinical context	Resettlement stress encompasses the challenges of meeting basic needs. Although many such stressors are not uniquely faced by immigrants and refugees (e.g., attaining housing, employment, and health care), challenges of language, acculturation, and loss of social capital contribute to basic needs being harder to meet. In addition, some immigrants contend with specific resettlement challenges such as seeking legal status.
Clinical implications	Families may be unable or unwilling to spend time and resources on seeking mental health care when basic needs are unmet; helping to address these needs through treatment and/or demonstrating how mental health care can help reduce resettlement stress and engage families in treatment.
What can providers and care systems do?	Clinicians can address resettlement stress through the following: *Integration:* Integrate mental health services with other social services. *Referrals:* provide a warm handoff to other service providers so that families feel their concerns have been heard and addressed. *Framing:* Identify ways in which mental health treatment can reduce resettlement stress (e.g., reducing the number of times a parent is called from work to take care of their child). *Holistic care:* Recognize that resettlement stressors may directly be contributing to a child's mental health problems and that addressing these stressors can be a part of good mental health care.

at the hands of authorities (Hynes, 2003). In countries that create forcibly displaced refugees and immigrants, those in power have systematically failed to protect their citizens and have, at times, perpetrated atrocities directly against them. Refugees may have lived for years under systems in which the government was corrupt and dangerous, in which those in power had access to brutal force, and in which sharing personal information, such as the name of one's tribe or the specifics of one's ethnic background, could mean certain death. Although to a clinician sitting in his or her office such atrocities may seem remote, they may be highly salient to a refugee contemplating bringing his or her child to a person in a relative position of authority. Some newer refugees and immigrants may not fully understand the distinction between mental health providers and child welfare agencies and may be concerned that bringing their child to psychological or psychiatric services may lead to their child's being removed from the home (Earner, 2007). Parents and families may question why a provider needs personal information and may either withhold information or give answers that they believe are "safe" (although, perhaps, not true). For instance, a question as simple as, "Are you the child's mother?" may be seen as an attempt to determine whether family members lied about their relationships in order to be resettled as a family (Griffiths, 2012). For immigrants without documented legal status, fears that providers will turn them in to Immigration and Customs Enforcement may prevent them from seeking out any care at all (Biswas, Kristiansen, Krasnik, & Norredam, 2011).

Concerns about safety and trust of authority figures and systems may inhibit the development of an effective and supportive therapeutic relationship or lead to refugees and immigrants failing to remain in treatment or avoiding services altogether (Colucci et al., 2015; Colucci, Szwarc, Minas, Paxton, & Guerra, 2014). Thus, a major legacy of the abuse and neglect that refugees often experience at the hands of authorities is the diminished access to needed care and services even after resettlement. Recognizing the power difference inherent in the therapeutic relationship, and how that relationship is shaped by historical experiences, is the beginning of building trust. Distrust of providers and the systems of care that they represent can impede access to care for clients and can negatively affect patient engagement, adherence to recommended treatment, and outcomes.

Although trust will be a reflection of the particular therapeutic relationship, various strategies can help to overcome immigrant and refugee families' distrust of authority. Trust-building can take time, particularly for families reticent to share information. Accepting a slower pace, and working to build trust through transparency, honesty, and actions that demonstrate reliability can lay the groundwork for a trusting relationship. (See Exhibit 3.2.)

BARRIER 3: STIGMA OF MENTAL ILLNESS

Think back to the vignette at the beginning of this chapter: One of the mother's first statements was, "My son is not crazy." Having mental health problems and seeking mental health services are stigmatized processes around the globe, and many traces of the shame and stigma associated with seeking mental health services still exist within the United States (Bharadwaj, Pai, & Suziedelyte, 2017). Many cultural groups hold a dichotomous view about psychological wellness that someone is either "mad" (e.g., experiencing acute psychosis) or "not mad," and there is little nuance between these two extremes. In many cultures, commonly used terms related to mental health, such as depression, anxiety, and attention deficit/hyperactivity disorder, do not exist (Betancourt, Abdi, et al., 2015). Instead, symptoms of mental

EXHIBIT 3.2. Distrust of Authority

Distrust of authority in the clinical context	Due to historical abuse by those in authority and differences in culture and beliefs, refugees might feel distrustful of those trying to provide services to them.
Clinical implications	Failure to recognize that one's position of authority may engender distrust, and/or failure to address/prioritize it early in the relationship, can result in client's refusal to seek/accept services or to share information.
What can providers do?	Trust is built through the following:
	Time: Accept a slower pace. Trust building takes time.
	Clarity: State clearly what each provider can and cannot do.
	Framing: Align the work with the client's values.
	Integrity: Never shy away from the difficult issues (e.g., acknowledge up front if a provider is a mandated reporter).
	Follow-through: Follow through on promises to clients. Show through actions that providers can be trusted.

health problems are considered signs of possession, personal or parental failure, or a punishment by God indicating that a transgression of faith has occurred (Alvidrez, 1999).

In countries where there is no formal system of mental health care, individuals with psychological disorders may have suffered horrific treatment, including violent restraint strategies, and those who have borne witness to this may, for good reasons, refuse to believe that anyone they love could similarly be suffering (Drew et al., 2011). The labels *mentally ill* or *mental health problem* may effectively communicate that someone has no hope of recovery and will suffer terribly. This is especially true when talking about children. Often, the motivation for refugee families to seek resettlement in the first place is the hope that their children will have a better future. Hearing that their child has a mental health problem might cause parents to feel as though all they have done to bring their children to a safe place has been for naught, and that they have failed, therefore, to protect their child. This, in turn, may undermine pride in one of their great achievements: protecting their child during the horrific experiences of war and migration.

It can be tempting for clinicians to think that people who do not seek care for their children because of the stigma of mental health problems simply need psychoeducation about the diagnosis or disorder. Clinicians may believe that once a refugee client understands mental health problems through a Western lens they will cease to fear both the diagnoses and treatment and, consequently, engage in services. What this approach fails to appreciate, however, is that stigma permeates whole communities and may shape how the community itself relates to a child believed to have emotional or behavioral health problems; a child may be ostracized, losing critical social support at a time when he or she needs it most (Ellis, Lincoln, et al., 2010). Thus, within tightly knit communities, the stigma of mental illness is not only about the *perception* that the label will hurt a child, but also the *reality* of what happens to entire family systems when such a culturally toxic label is applied to their child. Psychoeducation at the individual level alone will not change this; rather, broader shifts to change the acceptance of mental health care across entire communities are needed (Shannon, Wieling, Simmelink-McCleary, & Becher, 2015).

Failure to address the stigma of mental illness can lead to a refusal to engage in mental health services for fear of loss of social status and the shame of having a child who might be labelled as "crazy." Some strategies for addressing stigma operate at a systemic level; providing psychoeducation to the broader community and integrating mental health care into other care settings can diminish stigma and the associated barriers to engagement. In addition, individual providers can adopt multiple strategies to overcome the stigma of mental illness among their clients, including taking a strengths-based approach and using language and concepts that are culturally relevant to the client. (See Exhibit 3.3.)

BARRIER 4: LANGUAGE AND CULTURAL FACTORS

Language and cultural differences are among the most tangible barriers to engaging refugee youth and families in services (Scuglik, Alarcón, Lapeyre, Williams, & Logan, 2007). Although closely related, we will handle *language* and *cultural* barriers separately.

Language

An estimated 460 languages are spoken in homes throughout the United States (American Psychological Association [APA] Presidential Task Force on Immigration, 2012). As an illustration of the linguistic diversity that makes up communities heavily populated by immigrants, within a single school district in Portland, Maine, over 55 languages are spoken (Portland Public Schools, 2019). Although some refugees and immigrants are, or become, fluent in English, services need to be accessible to all.

EXHIBIT 3.3. Stigma

Stigma in the clinical context	*Stigma* is a mark that devalues or disgraces an individual in the eyes of his community or in his own estimation, here the label of "mentally ill."
Clinical implications	Having a child labeled as mentally ill can lead to shame, fear, and a sense of profound loss in some communities. A desire to avoid stigma can lead to families refusing services, hiding symptoms, or failing to follow through with the recommended treatment. The stigma associated with a mental illness diagnosis or attending treatment can lead to practical losses of social support (e.g., in some communities families may not want their child to associate with another child in the community who is known to have a mental illness).
What can providers do?	Stigma operates at both the individual and community levels; strategies to overcome stigma can be implemented at each of these levels as well:
	Embeddedness: Destigmatize mental health services by embedding them in more acceptable institutions such as education or concrete services.
	Asset-focused: Present mental health services in a positive rather than deficit-based framing (e.g., as a means to achieve valued educational goals or improve family functioning).
	Clarity: Avoid using psychological jargon that does not translate well; instead, use concrete examples of how the child and family can benefit from the services.
	Integration: Integrate cultural and community values that create agency, hope, and resilience.
	Education: Engage and educate the wider community. In particular, engage community opinion leaders as partners.

Although youth resettled in the United States often develop English language skills very rapidly, this can create new challenges. Full proficiency typically takes 8 years and may be more difficult for those who lack literacy in their native language or have gaps in formal education (V. P. Collier, 1995). Sometimes children lose or never develop full proficiency in their native language while parents continue to struggle to learn English. The result is a child who may not be fully proficient in *any* language and may not share a common proficient language with his or her parents. Making treatment accessible in the language that best fits both child and parent (which may or may not be the same) is a critical step for engagement.

Because children often develop English language skills more quickly than their parents, youth are sometimes put in the position of acting as a de facto interpreter for their parents. A child may be asked by their family to read mail from billing agencies or school, to set up appointments, and to take telephone calls from health care and social service providers. When a child is asked to interpret for a family within the therapeutic encounter, it can be harmful to both the child and the treatment process (Anguiano, 2018). Thoughtful organizational planning can ensure that in-person or phone interpretation is available during clinical encounters with non-English-speaking clients.

Cultural Differences

Culture includes language but more broadly encompasses beliefs, customs, and behaviors shared by a group of people. It encompasses everything from how people relate to each other, to the meaning they attach to experiences, and to whom they go to for help when in distress. Culture can be thought of as the lenses through which we see the world: Everything we see is framed, colored, and brought into focus according to our culture. Culture fundamentally shapes the way that families see and understand mental health problems and mental health services.

Different cultures have different explanatory models for why someone exhibits certain behaviors, and, correspondingly, the solutions they seek for them may having nothing to do with Western diagnostic categories and frameworks of psychological health and illness (Kleinman, 1980). If the problem of a child's nightmares is seen as a sign of spiritual malady, then the logical source of help will be a religious leader; sharing such problems with a health care provider or counselor may seem irrelevant and, indeed, odd. Moreover, using their own cultural lenses, parents have their own understanding of to what the child's symptoms should be attributed, whom to go to for these types of issues, what needs to be done to heal and support the child, and what the expected outcome should be. When clinicians offer a family an explanation of psychological illness, they are also using their own cultural lenses (from their training and their own cultural identity), which may be very different from the family's understanding. When recommending treatment or providing an assessment, clinicians must understand that there are several, even many, truths in the room.

Although mental health providers will never become experts in all languages and cultures, engaging refugee families requires that providers come to understand the processes by which language and culture shape thought, behaviors, and emotional reactions to mental health problems and mental health treatment, as well as how these factors can be addressed,

EXHIBIT 3.4. Linguistic and Cultural Barriers

Linguistic barriers in the clinical context	Linguistic barriers include not speaking English, absence of a trained interpreter in the care system, and use of idioms/concepts that are difficult to translate even in the presence of an interpreter. Cultural barriers include different explanatory models of symptoms between clients and providers, culturally specific help-seeking practices, and culturally bound symptom presentation (e.g., somatic presentation in certain communities). Cultural barriers also include belief systems around illness and healing and how and to whom to speak about psychological distress.
Clinical implications	Linguistic and cultural differences are often the primary reason that refugees do not seek mental health support. Refugees might not seek help because there is no one who speaks their language to facilitate access, or they might abandon care because they feel that the suggested treatment is not aligned with their cultural beliefs or their understanding of the problem.
What can providers do?	Providers can address linguistic and cultural barriers through the following:
	Education: Learn about the cultures of the communities being served.
	Reflection: Reflect on one's own culture and how it shapes one's approach to treatment and clients.
	Planning: Plan for better communication by engaging interpreters or cultural brokers, and work with them to understand a family's understanding of illness and healing.

integrated, appreciated, and understood as part of the engagement and treatment process. In Exhibit 3.4, we present strategies that can help providers to address linguistic and cultural barriers such as by learning about the cultures of the communities they serve, by reflecting on how their own culture shapes the way they practice, and by ensuring that there is linguistic and cultural support.

SYSTEMIC STRATEGIES FOR OVERCOMING BARRIERS AND ENGAGING FAMILIES

Truly overcoming barriers to engaging refugees in mental health treatment requires systemic and structural shifts in how care is delivered; some of the innovative and evidence-informed models that have successfully engaged refugees are described in Chapter 6 of this volume. Although systemic change may take months or even years, there are also significant steps that can be taken by individual providers in order to enhance the likelihood of successfully engaging refugee families. Strategies at each of these levels are described below.

Figure 3.1 illustrates four strategies that can successfully address the four barriers. Although each of the strategies most directly addresses the barrier to which it points, each strategy may also positively impact other barriers, and programs that combine all four strategies may likely facilitate the best possible outcomes. Ultimately it is the bringing together of ethnic community and service systems in genuine partnership that can most effectively address barriers to engagement.

Community Engagement

Refugee communities can be essential partners and allies in engaging refugee youth in services. Members of a community often hold a deep understanding

FIGURE 3.1. Barriers and Strategies for Engaging Refugee and Immigrant Families

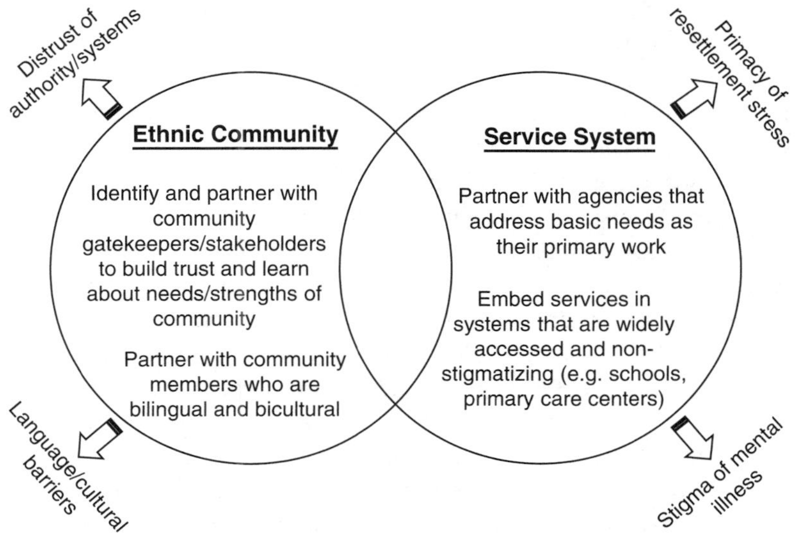

Key strategies (depicted in the circles) can be used to overcome barriers to engagement (depicted outside the circles). The left circle illustrates resources to be called upon from within ethnic communities, and the right circle illustrates resources to be called upon from the service system. Systemic strategies for overcoming barriers to treatment engagement fundamentally involve bringing together the refugee/immigrant ethnic community and the service system through integration, cross-learning and genuine partnerships.

of the needs of their community's youth, what would be perceived as helpful services, and who (within and beyond the community) should be trusted. *Gatekeepers* is a term that refers to natural leaders within a community who, because of their relational position with others, may be particularly influential in helping families into care (Ellis, Lincoln, et al., 2010). An approach to community engagement that respects community members as equal partners and honors the knowledge and expertise that they hold can lead to both valuable process and content in building a mental health program for refugees. A willingness to listen openly and honestly to community members and engage them as partners in developing programs and services may help diminish power differentials and build trusting relationships between community members and providers. Equally important, programs should be constructed in ways that are mindful of the cultural perspectives of community members and consistent with their values and approaches to healing.

For example, in Lowell, Massachusetts, a coalition focused on reducing cardiovascular disease and diabetes among Cambodian refugees successfully engaged the community through community outreach (Grigg-Saito, Och, Liang, Toof, & Silka, 2008). Specific strategies included door-to-door visits from health educators; building relationships with and distributing information through Cambodian business owners and businesses; and providing educational forums and "learning tours" to health care and other government and service organizations, an elders council, a faith-based outreach, and Tai Chi groups. The coalition also focused on learning from the Cambodian community and conducting outreach to non-Cambodian providers to help them better understand Cambodian culture and community needs. Over the course of the outreach program, the number of Cambodian patients accessing health care through the lead agency grew from none to more than 4,000, and many became trained as health workers and interpreters. In addition, nearly 1,000 health care providers received training in cultural competency (Grigg-Saito et al., 2008). This program demonstrates how genuine community engagement around a key health issue can lead to a transformation within both the refugee community and the provider community.

Practically, community engagement may take a range of forms. An agency or provider that seeks to serve refugees better could reach out to ethnic-based community organizations or refugee-resettlement agencies simply to meet informally with community members to learn about community concerns and to share information about services. These meetings may open the door to continued learning, engagement, and partnership; and, over time, trusting relationships may emerge. Regardless of the form it takes, successful community engagement means being open to learning and listening, respecting differences, and viewing community partners as equals in the work of helping children.

Clinicians can also seek to build trust and engagement individually by communicating clearly about their role and the fact that they operate separately from child welfare or law enforcement (Torres et al., 2018). For undocumented immigrants who fear deportation, this may be particularly important.

Embedding Services in Service Systems

One approach to overcoming the stigma of mental health services is to embed mental health care within service systems that are more commonly accessed and trusted by refugee communities. As described below, pediatric care centers and schools provide two examples of service systems that can be valuable settings for refugee youth mental health care.

Research suggests that schools tend to be trusted systems and seen by parents as "helpers" for their children (Ellis, Lincoln, et al., 2010). Often, framing treatment as something that will "help children succeed in school" speaks volumes to refugee parents, and mental health services in the context of the school are easily seen in this way. Refugee youth themselves have identified schools as natural places to seek support. In a study of Somali adolescents, the most frequent sources of support were family and school (Ellis, Lincoln, et al., 2010). In a study of adolescent refugees from diverse backgrounds attending school in the United Kingdom, the majority preferred seeking help through school over other options. Many reported that school felt safe and familiar, making it feasible and comfortable to meet with their therapist both during scheduled appointments and on an as-needed basis (Fazel, Garcia, & Stein, 2016). By contrast, hospitals and mental health clinics are often situated in unfamiliar locations and filled with strangers, making them less accessible and appealing to refugee youth. Although privacy emerges as a major consideration for school-based services, youth may ultimately feel less stigmatized by services that are received in school and organized around the goal of helping them succeed in that environment.

Mental health services offered in primary care settings have the advantage of more easily being understood as addressing a treatable health condition and as part of routine care. As a result, delivering mental health services embedded within a routine care setting can reduce some of the stigma associated with entering clinics that exclusively treat psychological problems or explicitly state *Psychiatric Clinic* on their signage (Shim & Rust, 2013). Additionally, many refugee youth may first present with psychological distress via somatic complaints (Westermeyer et al., 2010). If and when physical and medical ailments have been ruled out, mental health providers can use these somatic complaints as a way into conversations about psychological suffering. For examples, a clinician could say,

> Many children starting a new school may have stomach and headaches because of the stress and excitement of being at school—by working with a counselor, they can talk through these experiences and learn helpful skills to be successful and effective at school. As a result, they will also likely have fewer headaches, and if they do get headaches, will have some ways to manage them.

Partnering with Cultural Experts

As noted earlier, cultural brokers may serve many roles within effective refugee services, including as an interpreter. Whereas in some health care settings interpreters function as a mere conduit for communication between the identified client and provider, in other settings cultural brokers serve to enhance both linguistic and cultural understanding (Singh et al., 1999). The cultural broker acts as a bridge between the clinician and the patient, and by extension between health care institutions and the community, working toward creating greater understanding and a more collaborative relationship.

Programs That Provide a Range of Services

Earlier, we described the importance of addressing basic needs, such as financial or housing stress, as critical to engaging and treating refugees and immigrants. One example of a program that embeds social services within mental health services is the Program for Survivors of Torture (PSOT) at Bellevue in New York. After assessing clients' social service needs through a social ecological lens, the program assigns social services staff to work with the client around practical needs. The program provides services such as ESL and citizenship classes in-house, and also builds relationships with partner agencies that can provide services that are not available at PSOT (Physicians for Human Rights & Bellevue/NYU Program for Survivors of Torture, 2003). Efforts to address resettlement stress such as those implemented by PSOT serve the double function of both communicating to families that the therapist understands the importance of these needs and of reducing stress that, in and of itself, may be exacerbating mental health symptoms.

Let us now return to the story of the Somali boy whose referral to mental health was discussed in the beginning of this chapter and consider how his story might have played out in a system built around the principles we have described.

> The mother of a 9-year-old Somali boy arrives at school to pick up her son, who had stayed after school to attend a skills group. As the group emerges from the meeting room, laughing and chatting, a Somali woman who coleads the group waves the mother over. They exchange a greeting and pleasantries, catching up briefly about their families and community news. The group coleader then asks the mother if she has a few minutes to chat privately. The group coleader describes the boy's progress in the group but also shares that he was continuing to have trouble in the classroom and became upset earlier, knocking over desks. The coleader then shared that she had spoken with the teacher, who was worried, and wondered if they could meet together with the mother and the group's other coleader—a psychologist—to discuss how to help him succeed in the classroom. The coleader added that she knew the mother was managing a lot at home and it could be a good opportunity to talk about how they could support those needs as well. The mother nodded in agreement, and a meeting was set for the next day.

The vignette above reflects a fundamental integration of service systems and community, and the work of individuals deeply committed to improving mental health care for refugees and immigrants. Providers who want to serve refugees can take steps to make services more accessible, acceptable, and appropriate to the needs of this population. These steps can be at the provider level—for instance, developing cultural humility—or at the level of the system of care; for example, embedding cultural brokers in a services system. Working across these levels, barriers to engagement can be diminished and refugee children can more easily access the care they need to heal and flourish.

PSYCHOSOCIAL ASSESSMENT WITH REFUGEE AND IMMIGRANT YOUTH AND FAMILIES

4

Seven-year-old Rayhan, who immigrated from Syria several months ago, has been getting in trouble at school. In particular, teachers have noted that he gets aggressive in the cafeteria, shoving other kids in the lunch line. He often takes a very large lunch, and adults have noted that much of it is not eaten—in fact, he puts most of it directly into his backpack. He also is having trouble in his classroom. His teacher reports he sometimes seems "spaced out and disengaged" and other times seems "irritable and easily angered." He is not progressing adequately in his learning and schoolwork, and his teacher is worried about his ability to move to the next grade.

Understanding what drives the behavior of a refugee child or adolescent is often complex, sometimes confusing, and potentially overwhelming for even the most seasoned clinicians. A thoughtful, accurate, and culturally responsive assessment is invaluable in formulating and organizing a successful treatment plan. Consider the chapter's opening scenario, and then consider a few of the myriad explanations that could help explain some of Rayhan's behaviors:

Observed Behavior 1: "Gets aggressive in the cafeteria, shoving other kids in the lunch line."

http://dx.doi.org/10.1037/0000163-004
Mental Health Practice With Immigrant and Refugee Youth: A Socioecological Framework,
by B. H. Ellis, S. M. Abdi, and J. P. Winer

Possible explanations of this behavior (see Figure 4.1):

1. *Rayhan is experiencing current symptoms of posttraumatic stress disorder (PTSD):* Rayhan may be triggered by the noisy cafeteria, where a dropped plastic tray may sound like a gunshot and children laughing and squealing loudly may sound like cries for help.

2. *Social learning in different contexts taught Rayhan what was adaptive:* Rayhan grew up in refugee camps where shoving to the front of the food-distribution line was normative, necessary, and a highly adaptive means of survival.

3. *The behavior is a manifestation of Rayhan's acculturative stress:* Rayhan is not yet familiar with the norms and expectations of U.S. schools. In his culture of origin, roughhousing among male peers is normal and a way to show camaraderie; in the United States the same behavior leads teachers to state that he is acting "out of control."

4. *Rayhan's behavior is motivated by acute hunger:* Rayhan has inadequate food at home because of poverty.

Observed Behavior 2: "Takes a very large lunch . . . much of it not eaten . . . puts in backpack."
Possible explanations for this behavior:

1. *Social learning in different contexts taught Rayhan what was adaptive:* Hoarding food was normative and a means of survival in the refugee camp. Rayhan's mother would give him an extra-big hug if he came home with extra food for his little sisters. He may be attempting to assume the role of a provider or "bread winner" for family and friends.

2. *Rayhan is experiencing symptoms of depression:* He may have a suppressed and limited appetite but is nevertheless aware of the cultural importance of not wasting food.

Observed Behavior 3: "Having trouble in the classroom, sometimes seems 'spaced out and disengaged' and other times seems 'irritable and easily angered.' He is not progressing adequately in his learning and work."
This behavior could be explained by some of the same processes identified above as well as additional potential explanations that include:

1. *Rayhan has limited language fluency:* Rayhan may have poor language comprehension of what is going on in classroom, resulting in difficulty attending to material and poor academic performance.

FIGURE 4.1. Visual Representation of Sample Etiological Factors that Influence Observed Behavior of a Youth With a Refugee Background

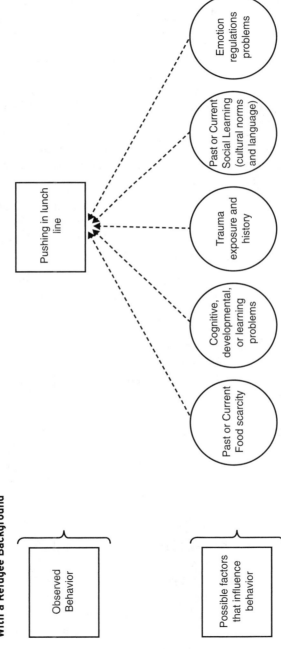

2. *Rayhan has significant gaps in previous formal education because of war and refugee camp experiences:* Rayhan may lack the base of knowledge that is assumed of children of his chronological age and grade level; consequently, he may feel frustrated and unable to progress.

3. *Rayhan has dissociative symptoms (including derealization or depersonalization) associated with past trauma exposure:* Rayhan may have difficulty staying grounded in the present moment and have difficulty processing and integrating new information effectively. He may become disengaged, frustrated, and perform poorly in academics.

4. *Rayhan has symptoms of a learning disability or difference:* Rayhan is unable to process classroom information effectively, leading to disengagement, frustration, and poor academic performance.

5. *Rayhan has symptoms resulting from a head injury or traumatic brain injury from physical trauma during war or migration:* This could lead to a diversity of emotional, cognitive, or intellectual difficulties (or all of these) that affect his mood and academic performance.

A clinician's treatment plan would vary greatly depending on which of the above formulations is seen as the primary problem. How is the primary problem determined? What if there is more than one problem driving the observed behaviors? How might the various problems be interacting, and how can they possibly be sorted out?

Although these questions have no easy answers, a clearer picture of what will be most effective in supporting the child and his or her social environment is possible with a thoughtful and thorough assessment of the child's history, culture, current environment, and cognitive and emotional functioning. In this chapter, we first discuss general clinical considerations related to the process of conducting assessments with refugee and immigrant children and adolescents. We then describe assessment challenges and recommendations in three sections: before the first session, during the first session(s), and over the course of treatment.

GENERAL CONSIDERATIONS IN ASSESSMENT

The mental health field has at times been criticized for the "overmedicalization" of human suffering by viewing experiences such as war and displacement through a lens that focuses too narrowly on trauma, PTSD, and psychiatric illness. For example, Summerfield (1999) cautioned against objectifying the "misery of war as a pathological entity apart (i.e., trauma)"; instead, he argued, "uprooted peoples do well or not as a function of their capacity to rebuild . . . sociocultural networks and a sense of community" (p. 1461). Papadopoulos (2007) similarly reminded us that being a refugee is a sociopolitical and legal phenomenon, rather than a psychological or medical state. Thus, although a thorough mental health assessment is indicated for any child—refugee, immigrant, or otherwise—who presents for mental health treatment, maintaining a broader lens on the whole child, the social environment, their unique strengths, and their capacities for resilience will help prevent the myopic assumption that trauma defines a displaced child's entire experience and functioning. Throughout treatment, it is important to consider the role that culture and personal history play in the lives of the family members and in the process of help seeking (e.g., Haslam, Jetten, Postmes, & Haslam, 2009), as well as in the strengths and resources that they bring to healing. Consider the following unaccompanied immigrant adolescent, whose story was shared by Baily, Henderson, and Tayler (2016) and is summarized here:

> Edwin is a quiet 16-year-old Salvadoran boy who migrated unaccompanied to the United States 2 years earlier. When he was 7 years old, his single mother, who struggled to make ends meet, migrated without authorization to the United States so that she could send money back to support him. Edwin lived with his grandmother, with whom he became very close. At school, Edwin was the target of vicious and at times violent bullying. After experiencing a serious assault, he formed a plan to leave El Salvador and join his mother in the United States. He travelled by foot to southern Mexico, and from there joined other unaccompanied children who traveled on "La Bestia," the notoriously dangerous freight train heading north. His journey was marked by hunger, homelessness, and interactions with corrupt officials, but also with kind gestures from strangers who helped him with both material and spiritual gifts. In describing his journey, he recalls these moments, and that he and others he traveled with "laughed a lot because we were family, and we told jokes" (Baily et al., 2016, p. 769). After crossing into the United States, he was apprehended by U.S. immigration officials, who facilitated his reunion with his mother. Joyful to be with him again, she was able to secure legal representation to argue his case. Although he struggled with depression and anxiety, his family and school provided support and connection to mental health services.

As Baily and colleagues (2016) articulated, themes of resilience, resources, and strength weave throughout Edwin's story. On a personal level, Edwin appears to possess a capacity for optimism, self-reflection, gratitude, and social connection. Interpersonally, he benefits from deep attachments both with his mother in his early years and then his grandmother; this attachment seems to carry over into his successful reunification with his mother later. At a systemic level, humane interactions with immigration officials and swift reunification with family, rather than detention, likely also contribute to more successful adjustment. Across these different levels of the social ecology, key resources and strengths contribute to more resilient processes for Edwin despite a past that was marked by trauma and disruption. Although he struggles with mental illness, he also is deeply engaged with his family and community and is on a path toward healing.

Throughout the assessment process, attention to strengths and resources can provide critical "leverage points" to build on in intervention. Assets such as secure attachments, psychological flexibility, respect for authorities and learning, strong family values, and the opportunity to take perspective across different cultures are just a few examples of important strengths that might be brought to bear on the healing journey of immigrant and refugee youth.

BEFORE THE FIRST APPOINTMENT: LAYING THE GROUNDWORK FOR A CULTURALLY RESPONSIVE SESSION

The first step in conducting an effective and culturally responsive assessment with refugees and immigrants can occur before they set foot in the office. A family's cultural background, as well as the recent historical context of that specific refugee or immigrant population, is valuable information of which to be aware, both for the sake of building rapport and to provide some context and depth to the story to be learned from the family. As Rechtman (2000) stated,

> Most of the refugees who have survived a given historical event share the same history with nearly the same trauma, the same loss, the same flight to escape, the same difficult resettlement and so on. Since the 'journey through death' began, each individual destiny seems to embody the group's collective fate. However, even if during the same period refugees have lived through quite the same events, this does not necessarily mean that they have experienced the same trauma. (p. 404)

Although every refugee and immigrant family's experience is unique, clinicians who educate themselves on a refugee population's culture, history, and the common events that engendered forced migration, enter the conversation and professional relationship with a better sense of what questions may be meaningful to ask and of how certain answers may be directly shaped by culture-specific processes (e.g., Isakson, Legerski, & Layne, 2015; Weine, 2015). Online resources (see the end of this chapter) can provide brief summaries of cultural norms, cultural perceptions and expressions of physical health and mental health, common refugee experiences, and typical resettlement patterns.

On the whole, clinicians should remember that families are to be looked to as experts in understanding their child's *specific* experiences; they should not be expected to provide a culture and history lesson to providers. There is a delicate line between appropriately asking youth and families to discuss and explain their specific past experiences and unfairly burdening them with the responsibility of educating a well-intentioned but naïve clinician on their cultural history. Learning basic information about a family's culture and their people's recent history can contribute to building trust and help to shape better clinical questions and formulation (Day-Vines et al., 2007; Sue & Sue, 2015). This learning should include an understanding of what caused the conflicts that drove families from their home country. Finally, on a most practical level, the provider must determine what languages the various family members are most comfortable speaking and arrange for an interpreter or cultural broker to be present who has experience with these languages. (See Exhibit 4.1.)

EXHIBIT 4.1. Clinical Assessment With Refugee and Immigrant Youth and Families: The What and the When

Things to Do Before the First Appointment
- Determine what language(s) the child speaks, what language(s) his or her parents or primary guardians speak, and what language(s) will be used in treatment.
- Determine what, if anything, has been communicated to the family about the clinician and/or organization.
- Read about sociopolitical events that occurred in the family's country of origin that may have contributed to the family's leaving the country.
- Identify/arrange for an interpreter or cultural broker.

Things to Do at the First Appointment(s)
- Determine the circumstances that led to the family's being referred, as well as the specific referral problem or question.
- Determine why the family thinks they are coming to the appointment, and what services or support they are seeking.
- Clarify what the clinician's job is and is not, as well as the value that mental health services can add.
- Determine whether the family's most basic needs are met: current safety, food, housing, health care, transportation?
- Begin to establish and develop trust and rapport.
- Evaluate the impact and severity of the four core stressors (resettlement, acculturation, isolation, and trauma; see Chapter 1).
- Identify strengths and resources

Things to Do Over the Course of Treatment
- Conduct a thorough mental health and/or psychological evaluation.

AT THE FIRST SESSION(S): BUILDING CONNECTION THROUGH ASSESSMENT OF CORE STRESSORS

Building rapport with families of different cultures can take time. Beginning the assessment process with a discussion of fundamental stressors and needs can help build a connection between the clinician and the family around practical, less stigmatized areas of need that are likely of high importance to the family. Thus, we recommend beginning the assessment process with a discussion of three of the four core stressors: resettlement, acculturation, and isolation. The Refugee Services Core Stressor Assessment Tool, an interactive refugee assessment tool developed at Boston Children's Hospital, may be accessed online at https://is.gd/Corestressortool.

The framing of an initial clinical assessment is a crucial moment that can either build rapport and enhance engagement or, if done poorly, ensure that a child or family will not return for treatment. Upon first meeting with a parent, child, or family, one potential way to frame your initial assessment, based on the four core stressors model, could include

> Over the course of our meetings, I want to do my best to understand what you and your family have been through, what is going well for you, and what is difficult. In order to do that, I will ask you about a lot of different experiences you may have had. I know this can be hard, so if there is anything I'm asking that you do not want to talk about, or you want to know why I am asking, please let me know. I may not be able to help with all the things you and your family are dealing with, but I would like to know as much as possible so that I can help you make the best plan.

Here, the clinician is seeking to (a) prepare the family for all the questions they will be asked, (b) ask the parents' or child's permission to ask these questions, (c) give the parent or child the agency and freedom to *not* answer certain questions, and (d) help them understand that the clinician may not be able to address everything they need help with.

In addition to the psychological consequences of witnessing or experiencing violence, the events that lead to forced migration are associated with a loss of numerous resources, as families leave behind homes and social networks and often expend their remaining resources during flight. This initial loss of resources significantly threatens the psychological well-being of children and families, further hampering their ability to retain or rebuild resources and social networks upon resettlement. The term *loss spirals* describes how resource loss can lead to mental health distress that may further affect resource loss (Betancourt, Abdi, et al., 2015; Heath, Hall,

Russ, Canetti, & Hobfoll, 2012). Effective interventions aim to disrupt and, ideally, reverse these loss spirals by promoting psychological health and the rebuilding of the network of financial and social resources that the family lost during forced migration. Thus, a full understanding of the various types of psychosocial stress experienced by displaced peoples can be helpful in several ways: building rapport by communicating to families that the provider is interested and attuned to the full range of experiences with which they struggle, promoting engagement by incorporating the management of foundational stressors (e.g., access to food and stable housing) as part of a treatment plan, and identifying social-environmental intervention targets that may be contributing to, or even driving, a child's mental health symptoms (e.g., K. E. Murray, Davidson, & Schweitzer, 2010). We now consider the assessment domains for each of the four core stressors.

Resettlement

The process of resettlement brings with it a number of stressors and challenges that may not be unique to resettlement but are often common among refugee and immigrant communities (Laban, Gernaat, Komproe, van der Tweel, & De Jong, 2005; Lindencrona, Ekblad, & Hauff, 2008). These resettlement stressors can be understood broadly as financial and logistical. *Financial stressors* may include poverty, inadequate or unstable housing, parental unemployment or underemployment, and expectations that a child or adolescent hold employment and bring home an income. *Logistical stressors* include challenges such as accessing effective public or private transportation and current legal statuses of the youths and their family members.

Minors who are detained after arriving in U.S. ports of entry may suffer the particularly egregious stressors of detention or family separation. Children who have been separated from their families face the stressors of resettlement or detention without the protective shield of their families and require special care in assessing their experiences and perceptions of what happened to them. Assessment of children held in detention centers, with or without family, also requires particular attention to the impact of the detention-center environment on the child's mental health and family relationships. In these situations, assessment of resettlement stress includes understanding the stress of the detention-center environment, legal uncertainty, and potentially compromised parenting because of either absence (in the case of family separation) or mental illness exacerbated by the detention process. (See Exhibit 4.2.)

EXHIBIT 4.2. Resettlement Stress: Questions to Guide Assessment

Basic Needs
- Is your family having trouble paying for basic necessities such as food, clothing, medication, and transportation?
- Is your family experiencing any current housing problems?
- Is your family's neighborhood safe?
- Is anyone in your family experiencing any threats to his/her immediate safety?

Health Care and Access to Services
- Does your family have access to regular medical, mental health, vision, and dental care?
- Is your family able to access transportation to important appointments?
- Do you feel your child is getting the help he/she needs to be successful at school?

Legal Status
- Does your family have a caseworker through a resettlement agency?
- Do you have any concerns about your family or family members being able to stay in this country legally?
- Do any of your family members need access to legal representation?

Special Considerations for Children Separated from Families or Held in Detention
- Was the child separated from family at the border? Does the child feel anger toward or blame parents or other adults for failing to provide adequate care and protection?
- If detained, what is the child's experience in detention? Does the child have access to information about his or her family, play space, learning opportunities, social support, and medical and psychological care?
- Who is the appropriate guardian to provide consent for evaluation and treatment? If a psychological assessment is conducted, how will the results be used, and who is it for?
- Who has access to the child's medical files, and can anything in these files be used to deny the child/family asylum?
- Is legal advocacy available to the family, and can the provider share resources to support the family's application for asylum?

Acculturation

Acculturative stress refers to the various types of stress that occur as a result of a child and family navigating between their culture of origin and the predominant culture of resettlement (e.g., Berry, 2005; Mena, Padilla, & Maldonado, 1987). The type and level of acculturation may vary with age, length of time in resettlement, and the "cultural distance" (e.g., the relative social and psychological differences in values and communication between two cultures) between the culture of origin and the culture of resettlement.

Different families may also adopt different stances toward acculturation. For instance, some may encourage integration into "mainstream" American culture and strive to speak English at home, whereas others may seek to protect their heritage culture and tightly maintain linguistic and cultural traditions in the home (Telzer, 2010). Some of these stressors may play out primarily between a child and his or her parents; for example, familial conflict over whether a child adopts new cultural values and behaviors, and parental fears of "losing" their child to the new culture. Other Acculturative stressors may take place in the school or community settings, where a child may struggle to fit in.

Importantly, some acculturative stress may be related to the internal psychology of defining one's identity and to the struggle to form an integrated identity that includes elements of both origin and resettlement cultures (Cohen & Kassan, 2018; Galliher, McLean, & Syed, 2017). Unique among refugee and immigrant populations is the fact that certain aspects of their identities may change over the course of migration and resettlement (Noels & Clément, 2015); children or parents may have once been "privileged" in one aspect of their identity that they now experience as more "marginalized." For example, for many youth growing up in the majority of countries in Africa, Black is the majority racial group; an African youth resettled in the United States may now be called "African American" and experience some of the sociocultural history, bias, and related experiences faced by Black youth in the U.S. context (Waters, 1994). Although a fuller understanding of a youth's sense of identity will emerge over the course of treatment, an initial assessment of both how the youth self-identifies and whether he or she experiences associated identity-based stress can aid in effectively tailoring treatment. (See Exhibit 4.3.)

Isolation

Isolation stress may be closely tied to acculturative stress but focuses more specifically on understanding a child and family's social relationships and connectedness. Social connection, a profoundly protective experience, almost by definition has been disrupted for refugee and immigrant families (Halcón et al., 2004; Kirmayer et al., 2011; Tyrer & Fazel, 2014). Two sides to isolation contribute to isolation stress: (a) the presence or absence of social connections both within one's ethnic community and beyond, and (b) experiences of discrimination, bias, stigma, and harassment.

Because immigration may involve temporary or permanent separations within families, social support at the level of family may be disrupted for

EXHIBIT 4.3. Acculturative Stress: Questions to Guide Assessment

Acculturation Gap Between Child and Parents/Guardians
- What do you think about U.S. culture? What about your family's culture of origin?
- When you argue with your child or parent, what do you argue about?
- What, if any, cultural differences have been a source of stress? What, if any, cultural differences have been a source of strength?
- Do you feel embarrassed or ashamed about your child or parents/guardians' attitudes, behaviors, or beliefs?
- Do you worry that any of your family members are "too American?"

Language
- Do you have someone to help you translate important documents/appointments if needed?
- Is your child picking up English as fast as his/her siblings, or does he or she seem to be having trouble with it?
- Are you (if age appropriate) and your family able to navigate the city on your own (e.g., read signs, take public transportation)?

Parenting Capacity
- What would make raising your child easier in the United States?
- Do you feel so stressed that it is difficult to spend time with your child?
- Do you feel like you understand some of the basic information about how your child's school works; for example, how and when to meet with your child's teachers?
- Do you understand how some of the parenting rules (e.g., you are not allowed to hit or physically hurt your child) in the United States are different from rules in other countries? Do you feel like you have strategies that work when your child is misbehaving?

some children; reunification, in addition to separation, may be a stressful process for families. For instance, in a study of immigrant adolescents from Asia, the Caribbean, Mexico, and Central America, 75% had been separated from at least one parent for a significant period of time (6 months–10 years); longer periods of separation were associated with more complicated family-reunification processes and higher levels of psychological symptoms (Suárez-Orozco, Bang, & Kim, 2011). Unaccompanied children who are in the custody of Office of Refugee Resettlement and live in an institutional facility may lack any family support; those in foster care may be living with unfamiliar people and in an unfamiliar culture. A thorough assessment of the child's past and present experiences of family separation, the potential for reunification, and the child's current living situation will provide critical information about potential strain or support in the child's life.

Xenophobia and discrimination significantly affect the mental health and well-being of immigrant and refugee youth (Williams & Mohammed, 2009).

Discrimination may be related to race, ethnicity, religion, or being an immigrant. These experiences can both directly impact adjustment of youth and indirectly contribute to diminished access to opportunities and social connection. (See Exhibit 4.4.)

Managing certain types of stressors (e.g., problems with housing, transportation, food access, and immigration-related paperwork) may not always be thought of as central to the work of mental health clinicians, especially those trained as psychotherapists as opposed to case managers. This noted, a good understanding of the full range of stressors that refugee and immigrant youth and families are experiencing is critical to understanding what drives their behaviors, thoughts, emotions, and overall functioning. Furthermore, addressing these stressors—either directly in treatment or through connecting families to the right resources and other providers—can profoundly improve both treatment engagement and psychosocial outcomes (e.g., Li, Liddell, & Nickerson, 2016). In sum, the four core stressors commonly affect refugee and immigrant youth and families and their psychological treatment; thoughtfully and strategically addressing these four core stressors can prevent or interrupt the loss spirals that are so common among these communities.

EXHIBIT 4.4. Isolation: Questions to Guide Assessment

Informal Social Support
- Do you or your child feel lonely a lot of the time?
- Do you or your child have close friends or family members with whom you or your child feel comfortable talking with?
- Do you or your child spend a lot of time alone, even when social interaction is desired?
- Do you or your child feel like "no one understands me?"
- Are you separated from important family members?

Formal Social Support
- Are you or your child involved with peer, social, or interest groups outside of school or work (e.g., athletic teams, religious groups, social clubs)?
- Do you or your child have any adults at school or work (e.g., teacher, supervisor, guidance counselor) who are helpful and supportive to you?
- Are there any community agencies that have been helpful to your family?

Discrimination, Stigma, and Bias
- Do you or your child experience discrimination, stigma, or unfair bias at school, work, or in your neighborhood?
- Do you or your child experience harassment from law enforcement, neighbors, or other individuals?
- Do you or your child get teased by people who are native to the United States?

Trauma

Although *trauma* needs to be understood as only one potential element of a refugee or immigrant child's experience, given the potentially high levels of exposure to violence, psychosocial assessment should include a formal trauma assessment. Two common (and opposing) mistakes in trauma assessment of refugees include (a) using a trauma-screening tool that focuses exclusively on the common kinds of experiences that occur in the United States and that misses common wartime trauma (Kaltman, Hurtado de Mendoza, Gonzales, Serrano, & Guarnaccia, 2011), and (b) focusing exclusively on trauma as something that occurred prior to resettlement, and missing potential current and ongoing neighborhood or family trauma that has occurred in resettlement. Indeed, postresettlement trauma is dishearteningly common among refugee and immigrant youth (e.g., Apfel & Simon, 1996; Betancourt, Abdi, et al., 2015). Some types of trauma exposure can occur across any of the migration phases—for example, physical abuse, sexual abuse, or injury. In Exhibit 4.5 we highlight specific types of trauma that may be unique to, or more common within, the various phases of migration.

The relative value of knowing the extent and type of trauma exposure must be weighed against the potentially upsetting process of describing a difficult past history. Because whole families often experienced significant trauma together, the clinician should note that parents may be describing their own past trauma when talking about their child's experiences. The assessment of trauma with unaccompanied children presents a different set of challenges, as children may be developmentally unable to provide an accurate description of what they have been through or may be particularly emotionally vulnerable without parental support.

ASSESSMENT OVER THE COURSE OF TREATMENT: MENTAL HEALTH AND PSYCHOLOGICAL ASSESSMENT

Psychological assessments that are conducted cross-culturally face two immediate challenges to validity. First, although all cultures have ways of describing psychological distress, the specific terms, symptoms, and diagnoses common in Western-based discussions of mental health may not be applicable and may require adjustment. For example, some mental health–specific terms (e.g., *depression, anxiety, PTSD, ADHD, intrusive thoughts, insomnia, self-harm*) may have no direct or clear translation in some languages or may carry a different level of meaning. Different cultures exhibit and explain psychological symptoms in various ways. Cultural idioms

EXHIBIT 4.5. Trauma Across Migration

Premigration
- War and conflict exposure
  - Torture
  - Gang violence
  - Oppressive military or government practices
- Natural disaster

Migration
- Long and dangerous travel (including long distances by foot, crowded/unsafe vehicles or boats, dangerous rides on cargo trains)
- Chronic lack of shelter and food
- Smuggling and extortion by "coyotes" (persons who coordinate the movement of migrants over borders)
- Living in a refugee camp (often with dangerous circumstances; e.g., violence or fires)
- Being held in a detention center
- Sex trafficking
- Sexual assault
- Kidnapping

Resettlement
- Community violence
- Gang violence
- Hate crimes
- Family separation
- Threatened/actual deportation

---

of distress—meaning culture- and context-specific expressions or symbols of psychological suffering—may be helpful points of consideration when conducting assessments (Betancourt, Frounfelker, et al., 2015; Dein & Illaiee, 2013; Im, Ferguson, & Hunter, 2017; Kleinman, 1991; Kleinman, Eisenberg, & Good, 2006). For example, two distress-related syndromes that may be commonly exhibited among refugee and immigrant clients of Latinx backgrounds are *ataque de nervios* and *sustos*. Ataques de nervios are symptomatically similar to panic attacks but may also include acute anger, grief, suicidal or violent behavior, or dissociation, and can last for hours or multiple days (American Psychiatric Association, 2013; Moitra, Duarte-Velez, Lewis-Fernández, Weisberg, & Keller, 2018). Sustos, an "attack of the spirit," may entail a diversity of anxiety and somatic symptoms that unfold as a result of experiencing or witnessing an emotionally traumatic event (Razzouk, Nogueira, & Mari, 2011).

The fifth edition of the *Diagnostic and Statistical Manual of Mental Disorders* (*DSM–5*) has cross-cultural variations in presentations, giving more detailed information about cultural concepts of distress and explanations, and includes a 16-item Cultural Formulation Interview (American Psychiatric Association, 2013). The Cultural Formulation Interview is a helpful tool for understanding how cultural groups experience, understand, and communicate suffering and behavioral problems. It allows clients to define their distress in their own words. When possible, it is important to be as functionally and behaviorally descriptive as possible, so that, together, the clinician and family can build shared language. For instance, instead of asking, "Do you think your son is depressed?" a clinician might ask, "Do you think your son spends a lot of time looking and feeling sad?" Although parents might not know about Western mental health concepts, they will be able to speak to how their child is different from other children or how they were before. Asking parents, "Tell me how similar or different your child's development and behavior is compared with other children in your family," gives parents clear benchmarks that they can understand, and, consequently, better enable them to report on their child's behavior, affect, and developmental milestones.

A second challenge to validity in assessment of refugees is that many standardized psychological assessment tools have not been adapted, translated, and validated for diverse languages and cultures; this is particularly true for refugee children under the age of 6 (Gadeberg, Montgomery, Frederiksen, & Norredam, 2017). Cultural differences can contribute to false positives (identifying a problem that's not actually there) and false negatives (not identifying a problem that is actually there) in psychological assessment with refugee families. For example, asking, "Does your child often set fires?" might be seeking to identify a symptom that is associated with externalizing behavior problems or callous-unemotional traits in a Western context, but that could be positively endorsed by a parent from another culture where lighting fires (whether for preparing food or as religious observance) is seen as a daily and healthy life skill for children. During assessment, encourage children and families to provide observable examples of behaviors whenever possible, and this plus clinical judgment can improve interpretation of assessment results. Furthermore, certain quantitative assessment formats, such as responding to a question with a 1 to 7 Likert scale from *never* to *always*, may be unfamiliar to many refugees. Scales that use color gradients or shapes of increasing size superimposed on the traditional Likert scale can support effective assessment for families with low literacy or familiarity with Western self-report measures (Gadeberg et al., 2017; see Exhibit 4.6).

When scoring questionnaires and assessment batteries, it is important to remember that research-established norms and clinical cutoff scores may not be valid across different cultures (Sousa & Rojjanasrirat, 2011). When

EXHIBIT 4.6. Clinical Practice Recommendations in Using Structured Assessments With Refugee and Immigrant Youth and Families

- When possible, use instruments translated and validated for the culture of the child.

- If the above is not available, seek to provide the instrument/test in the preferred language of the child. Determine prior to the assessment session how and by whom the tool will be interpreted or translated.

- Always interpret results of the instrument/test in the context of information from other sources

  - This may occur in situations where a clinician has strong reason to believe a score may represent a *false positive* of symptoms. For example, "On the day of the assessment there had been a fire alarm at school and Rayhan's teacher reported this had been very distressing and disruptive for Rayhan. As a result, self-report measures assessing anxiety and PTSD may have been lower if assessed on a different day."

  - This may occur in situations where a clinician has strong reason to believe a score may represent a *false negative* of symptoms. For example, "In Rayhan's culture of origin, Syria, symptoms of anxiety may often be expressed through the description of physical symptoms (e.g., stomachache, headache, fatigue); as a result, measures of anxiety that focus more on the cognitive (i.e., 'I worry a lot'), as opposed to physiologically aspects of anxiety (i.e., 'My stomach hurts'), may not accurately capture the severity of Rayhan's anxiety symptoms."

- If nonvalidated tools are used, clearly state that they are to be used as a guide to clinical thinking rather than to provide definitive diagnostic information.

- Make the *rationale* and *function* of an assessment tool explicit and transparent. "Rayhan was administered our clinic's standard child anxiety measure, which is given to all new clients at admission. To our knowledge this measure has never been formally used or tested among youth of Arabic-speaking backgrounds and was administered through an Arabic-speaking phone interpreter of an Egyptian background. Although the measure indicates Rayhan may have clinically significant symptoms of anxiety, further culturally informed assessment of anxiety is indicated before a diagnosis can be made."

possible, instruments that have demonstrated cross-cultural validity for the specific population of interest should be used. If a cross-culturally valid instrument is not available, an assessment tool can still be used, but interpretation of the results should be conducted in the context of other psychosocial and cultural information and used to guide clinical thinking rather than determine diagnoses. Additionally, any psychological report using such a measure should clearly state the limitations of such a measure so as not to create a false sense of confidence in specific findings.

In Table 4.1 we provide evidence-based suggestions of psychological assessment measures that have been used with a variety of refugee and immigrant populations. Depending on need, we provide recommendations for single measures as well as larger and longer measures that are more

TABLE 4.1. Evidence-Informed Clinical Assessment Measures for Use With Refugee and Immigrant Youth

Measure	Domain	Age	Format	Languages
Beck Anxiety Inventory (BAI) (Beck, Epstein, Brown, & Steer, 1988)	Anxiety	13–80	21-item self-report, 10 minutes	Nepali, Arabic, and multiple other languages
Beck Depression Inventory–II (BDI–II) (Beck, Steer, & Brown, 1996)	Depression	13–80	21-item self-report, 5 minutes	Spanish, Arabic, and multiple other languages
Patient Health Questionnaire–9 (PHQ-9) (Spitzer, Kroenke, Williams, & the Patient Health Questionnaire Primary Care Study Group, 1999)	Depression	11+	9-item self-report, 3 minutes	Somali, Nepali, Arabic, and many other languages
Child Trauma Screening Questionnaire (Kenardy, Spence, & Macleod, 2006)	Posttraumatic Stress Disorder	6–18	10-item self-report, 3 minutes	Arabic, Burmese, Farsi, Indonesian, Mandarin, Nepali, Somali, and Vietnamese
UCLA Post-Traumatic Stress Disorder Reaction Index (DSM-IV; UCLA-PTSD) (Steinberg, Brymer, Decker, & Pynoos, 2004)	Posttraumatic Stress Disorder	6–18	22-item self-report, 20 minutes	English
Child and Youth Resilience Measure (Ungar & Liebenberg, 2011)	Resilience	Versions for: 5-9 (12 items) 10-23 (12 items) 9-23 (28 items)	Self-report, 5–10 minutes depending on age and version	English
Acculturative Hassles Index (AHI) (Vinokurov, Trickett, & Birman, 2002)	Acculturative stress	14–18	Self-report, 15 minutes	English
Bicultural Stressors Scale (Romero & Roberts, 2003)	Acculturative stress	11–15	Self-report, 5 minutes	English
Postmigration Living Difficulties (PMLD) (Silove, Sinnerbrink, Field, Manicavasagar, & Steel, 1997)	Resettlement stressors	18+	24-item self-report, 10 minutes	Arabic, Bengali, Chinese, French, Italian, Portuguese, Romanian, and Spanish

Measure	Construct	Age	Administration	Language
Postwar Adversities Index (Layne et al., 2010)	Resettlement stressors	11-20	23-item self-report, 10 minutes	English
Every Day Discrimination (EDD) (Williams, Yu, Jackson, & Anderson, 1997)	Discrimination	18+	9-item self-report, 5 minutes	English
Comprehensive psychological assessment measures				
Child Behavior Checklist (CBCL) (Achenbach & Rescorla, 2001)	Multiple subscales	Versions for: 1.5-5, 6-10, 11-18	Caregiver or teacher report on child functioning	Arabic, Swahili, Nepalese, and many others
Youth Self Report (YSR) (Achenbach & Rescorla, 2001)	Multiple subscales	11-18	112-item self-report, 25 minutes	Arabic, Swahili, Nepalese, and many others
Strengths and Difficulties Questionnaire (Goodman, Meltzer, & Bailey, 1998)	Multiple subscales	Versions for caregiver/educator report: 2-4, 4-10, 11-17; Self-report: 11-17, 18+	25-item self-report, caregiver report, and teacher report, 25 minutes	Arabic and multiple other languages
Measures for assessing parental symptoms				
Harvard Trauma Questionnaire (HTQ) (Mollica et al., 1996)	Posttraumatic Stress Disorder	18+	16-item self-report, 10 minutes	Arabic, Vietnamese, and many other languages
Hopkins Symptom Checklist (HSCL) (Parloff, Kelman, & Frank, 1954)	Subscales for depression and anxiety	18+	25-item self-report, 10 minutes	Arabic, Vietnamese, and many other languages

Note. This table highlights measures that are commonly used in research and clinical settings and that have been validated with ethnically diverse, war-exposed populations. A comprehensive list of measures for immigrant refugee youth and families can be found at https://www.nctsn.org/resources/measures-are-appropriate-refugee-children-and-families. From "'Measures That Are Appropriate for Refugee Children and Families,'" by National Child Traumatic Stress Network, 2015 (https://www.nctsn.org/resources/measures-are-appropriate-refugee-children-and-families). Adapted with permission.

comprehensive, but that may be more difficult to integrate into existing assessment batteries or standardized organizational tools. For further lists of addition measures that may be effective with refugee and immigrant youth and families, see Davidson, Murray, and Schweitzer (2010); Gadeberg et al. (2017); and National Child Traumatic Stress Network (2015).

In addition to the measures described in Table 4.1, a suite of measures, the Refugee Mental Health Assessment Package, was developed by Tay and colleagues to capture common refugee experiences and associated mental health problems (Tay et al., 2015). As of this writing, however, there is no well-established comprehensive battery of measures for refugee and immigrant youth.

Neuropsychiatric and Cognitive Testing

One particularly challenging area of assessment with refugee and immigrant youth is neuropsychiatric and cognitive testing. Recall the example at the beginning of the chapter of the boy who struggled with school work, inattention, hyperactivity, aggressive behavior, and low mood; a critical diagnostic question for him is whether he struggled with his school work because of one or more psychological disorders (e.g., PTSD, attention-deficit/hyperactivity disorder, depression), language problems, gaps in education, learning or cognitive difficulties, or some combination of the these problems. Although a neuropsychological assessment would typically be an important aid to answering these questions, the validity of neuropsychological tests with refugees is not yet well understood (Kaplan, Stolk, Valibhoy, Tucker, & Baker, 2016; Veliu & Leathem, 2017). Cognitive assessments such as the Weschler Intelligence Scale for Children (WISC–IV and WISC–V) have been normed across multiple ethnocultural groups and in multiple languages through the United States and around the world. However, there are no currently available clinical norms for youth from many of the countries with the largest populations of forced migrants (Gregoire et al., 2008; Wechsler, 2014). A child who is not fully fluent in English may score poorly on sections of tests that rely heavily on verbal ability (Suzuki & Ponterotto, 2008). Furthermore, forcibly displaced children may have acquired a number of languages across their lives, especially if they have spent time in several countries during their displacement and resettlement journey (Brown, Miller, & Mitchell, 2006; Kaplan et al., 2016). A thoughtful and sensitive assessment of current language abilities, including level of proficiency, is an important place to start in order to determine which and how much further neuropsychological testing should be administered and structured. The Bilingual

Verbal Ability Test (BVAT; Muñoz-Sandoval, Cummins, Alvarado, & Ruef, 2005), currently available in 17 languages, is one such tool that may assist with this process. Furthermore, although nonverbal psychological assessment measures may provide a general estimate of intelligence or academic capabilities, providers should be aware that even nonverbal measures may be biased by context, culture, and prior experience and may paint an inaccurate picture of a child's abilities (Kaplan et al., 2016).

In addition to language proficiency, other aspects of neurocognitive tests may be particularly influenced by cultural knowledge, such as U.S. political history or aspects of popular culture (Suzuki & Ponterotto, 2008), content that may be unfamiliar to a child born and raised outside of the United States. Culture may shape a child's understanding of how objects are used and the meaning they hold; for instance, past research has documented that Liberian children engaging in a card-sorting task tended to group "potato" and "knife" together because one was cut by the other and they thought it silly to group them separately as "foods" and "tools" (see Greenfield, 1997). Social norms (especially how children interact with adults and elders) may affect testing behavior. For example, refugee and immigrant youth from some cultures may feel it is inappropriate to ask clarifying questions of an authority figure even if something is unclear (Kaplan, 2009). Thus, although neuropsychiatric testing may provide some information about a child's abilities and cognitive functioning, results must be interpreted with caution and awareness of a child's cultural and linguistic background. Concurrent test translation by an interpreter during a psychological assessment has been strongly discouraged by some researchers because of potential for interpreter error (Casas et al., 2012; Kaplan, 2009; Kaplan et al., 2016). However, because of limited availability of bilingual psychologists and of translated and culturally validated tests in all possible languages, cognitive tests sometimes need to be administered with an interpreter (Searight & Searight, 2009). Results should be interpreted in the context of a comprehensive assessment that includes collateral information and be interpreted with significant caution. Further guidelines on conducting psychological assessments with interpreters can be found in Miletic et al. (2006) and Rousseau, Measham, and Moro (2011).

Asylum Evaluations

Clinicians working with refugee and immigrant youth may be called upon to conduct an asylum evaluation or provide treatment services specifically for asylum-seeking youth. Youth who are seeking asylum are individuals who are seeking international protection but whose refugee-status claims have not yet been verified. As such, they are working toward gaining legal status after they arrive in a country of resettlement and must demonstrate that their fear of persecution in their home country is well-founded. Because there is uncertainty around legal status in a country of resettlement, concerns about deportation are often very high. Matters are further complicated if youth are seeking asylum without a parent or guardian or have been intentionally and harmfully separated from a parent or guardian through a detainment process (Miletic et al., 2006; Torres Fernández, Chavez-Dueñas, & Consoli, 2015).

Providing a psychological assessment to accompany an asylum application that formally documents and/or substantiates claims of persecution and trauma can make the difference between a person being granted safe haven in a country of resettlement and being forcibly returned to a country where they were persecuted, harmed, or even tortured. During asylum evaluations mental health providers often work in tandem with the immigration attorney representing the child or family. When implemented effectively, asylum evaluations may function as a multifaceted intervention: (a) providing *assessment* of current psychological functioning and substantiating reports of persecution, via client report, of current suffering; (b) providing *advocacy*, as many asylum seekers are marginalized and victimized because of their identity and experience and are seeking safety; and (c) providing brief *intervention*. The process of conducting an asylum evaluation necessitates evoking a client's trauma narrative, which may be painful and dysregulating for trauma survivors (Gangsei & Deutsch, 2007). If conducted in a safe, strengths-based, and thoughtful manner, an often painful experience can be the start to a reauthoring experience in which a client becomes the empowered owner of his or her story, not just the victim of it.

Further information on formal training and webinars in conducting asylum evaluations is available through Physicians for Human Rights, a Nobel Prize–winning organization that conducts regular trainings for volunteer health professionals interested in conducting asylum evaluations. In addition, foundational guidelines for conducting an evaluation of an individual who reports experiences of torture are outlined in the United Nations' *Istanbul Protocol: Manual on the Effective Investigation and Documentation of Torture and Other Cruel, Inhuman or Degrading Treatment or Punishment.* (See the links to both resources at the end of this chapter.)

In sum, a thorough and thoughtful assessment is critical to arriving at the most effective treatment plan, as with any child. With refugee children, additional context around culture and social context may inform both the focus and interpretation of the assessments. Additional time may be needed to build the trust and rapport necessary to be able to assess all the relevant experiences and domains. In addition, incorporating an interpreter or taking the time to help explain the assessment process or Western psychological concepts and tools (e.g., use of numbered scales to rate experiences) are important and may understandably slow down the assessment process. Effective assessment with refugee and immigrant youth and families often requires the incorporation of new information, as it is learned and obtained, over the course of treatment. Importantly, prolonged assessment without any concrete intervention plans may frustrate parents and families who are still seeking to understand whether mental health services can be of value to their family. Working to address concrete ecological stressor needs *during* the assessment phase may serve both to address stressors and to demonstrate value to the family, thus facilitating rapport. This may also help to clarify the source of a child's problems. Recall Rayhan from the beginning of this chapter: Addressing the problem of hunger should not wait until the end of assessment. Immediate food assistance may forge trust between the provider and family and allow for an iterative assessment in which Rayhan's behavior can be reexamined with hunger removed from the equation.

LIST OF RESOURCES

Online resources for learning about culture and history of immigrants and refugees:

- http://ethnomed.org/
- http://www.culturalorientation.net/learning/backgrounders

Information and tools for conducting general psychosocial assessment with refugee and immigrant populations:

- Refugee Core Stressor Assessment Tool: an online measure that guides assessment of the Four Core Stressors and provides tailored recommendations for interventions: https://is.gd/Corestressortool
- A list of measures deemed appropriate for use with refugee youth by the National Child Traumatic Stress Network: http://nctsn.org/content/refugee-mental-health-measures
- Measures recommended by the Children and War Foundation: childrenandwar.org/measures/

Information and tools for conducting torture evaluations with refugees and immigrant populations:

- *Istanbul Protocol: Manual on the Effective Investigation and Documentation of Torture and Other Cruel, Inhuman or Degrading Treatment or Punishment*: https://www.ohchr.org/Documents/Publications/training 8Rev1en.pdf

- Physicians for Human Rights: https://phr.org/

- Physicians for Humans Rights, Trainings and Webinars for Health Professionals: https://phr.org/issues/asylum-and-persecution/asylum-network-trainings/

5

OUTPATIENT SOCIOECOLOGICAL AND TRAUMA TREATMENTS WITH REFUGEE AND IMMIGRANT YOUTH AND FAMILIES

Stressors affecting the mental health and adjustment of refugee and immigrant children and adolescents often span the social ecologies in which they live (Bronfenbrenner, 1979; Fazel, Reed, Panter-Brick, & Stein, 2012). Accordingly, treatment that integrates services across the layers of the social ecology is often indicated. At times, this can be accomplished by a clinician making appropriate referrals; at other times, clinicians may integrate these service elements directly into their treatment approach. Whereas Chapter 6 of this volume describes models of care for refugees and immigrants that are specifically designed to be collaborative and multidisciplinary in nature, in this chapter we focus on outpatient and trauma-focused models of care that have been effectively implemented by individual providers working with refugee youth and families. Because the core stressors of acculturation, isolation, and resettlement stress may all drive a child's symptomatology, developing a targeted plan to address these socioecological stressors in addition to mental health symptoms is an essential part of effective treatment. In the first part of this chapter, we provide suggestions for how a clinician can work to reduce socioecological stressors. Whereas addressing socioecological stressors alone may be sufficient for mental health improvement in some refugee

http://dx.doi.org/10.1037/0000163-005
Mental Health Practice With Immigrant and Refugee Youth: A Socioecological Framework,
by B. H. Ellis, S. M. Abdi, and J. P. Winer

children and adolescents, others will benefit from further trauma-focused intervention (Ellis et al., 2013). In the second part of this chapter we present specific trauma-focused models of care that can be used to address trauma-related mental health problems among refugee children and families.

SOCIOENVIRONMENTAL STRESSORS

A common assumption is that a refugee child presenting for mental health treatment needs trauma-focused treatment. Although children who have experienced war, displacement, and dangerous migrations certainly need trauma-*informed* treatment, trauma-*focused* treatment (e.g., treating symptoms directly associated with traumatic stress/posttraumatic stress disorder) may not necessarily be the place to start. Other socioenvironmental stressors may be critical factors in a child's functioning (Fitzsimons, Goodman, Kelly, & Smith, 2017) and may offer a more acceptable way for an outsider to become involved in helping a child and family. In some cases, problems that initially look like trauma-related mental health problems may dissipate once socioenvironmental stressors are attended to (Ellis et al., 2013). Thus, we recommend addressing the four core stressors (trauma, acculturation, isolation, and resettlement) as central and integrated components of a treatment plan.

To anchor our discussion of the importance of addressing the four core stressors, consider the case example of Rayhan in Chapter 4. After a careful assessment, Rayhan's outpatient therapist developed the following formulation:

> A past history of violence exposure and current symptoms of PTSD led to Rayhan's aggressive behavior and emotional dysregulation in school, particularly in chaotic or noisy settings such as the cafeteria (*traumatic stress*). Food insecurity related to family financial instability at home likely compounds his stress during lunch hour (*resettlement stress*). Given his recent arrival in this country, he also lacks an understanding of culturally influenced behavioral expectations within the school setting; this may contribute to his inappropriate behavior in the cafeteria (*acculturative stress*). In spite of these challenges, he is a very engaging and friendly boy who seems eager to build friendships (although, as yet, he is not able to identify any particular children as friends). Also, at times, other students make fun of his accent and his appearance (*isolation stress*). (See Figure 5.1.)

As can be seen in this formulation, all of the four core stressors may be important areas for intervention and support. Concentrating solely on trauma-focused treatment would fail to address important stressors that

FIGURE 5.1. Rayhan's Treatment Plan As Organized by the Four Core Stressors

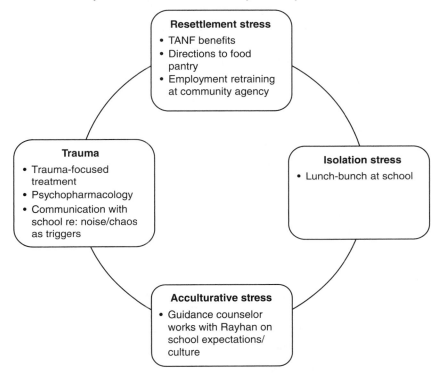

contribute to Rayhan's well-being; even if treatment reduced some of Rayhan's PTSD symptoms, other factors might continue to drive behavioral, affective, and adjustment problems. Thus, effective treatment for Rayhan will require attention to the full range of stressors and needs. Clinicians who are not embedded in an integrated care system can accomplish this in one of two ways: by facilitating effective referrals to other service providers or by providing direct intervention in the social environment (or both). Considerations related to each of these approaches are described next.

Addressing core stressors through referrals to other providers has the advantage of potentially engaging providers who have particular expertise in the identified areas of need. For instance, a housing advocate may be well-versed in the rights of and benefits available to families in need of housing, as well as in the best way of working within the system to help a family find safe and affordable housing. However, simply providing a referral name and number may prove ineffective in engaging a refugee family with the needed service. Just as with mental health services, barriers of distrust, uncertainty of the value and nature of the service, and cultural and linguistic barriers may inhibit engagement with new providers. In addition, coordinating with many different service providers, each of whom may have their own paperwork, intake processes, and professional procedures, may be confusing and overwhelming for families.

A clinician can seek to mitigate these challenges in a number of ways. One approach is to act as a bridge to new providers (e.g., Ayón, 2014). Facilitating a phone call, attending or hosting a first meeting between the family and another provider, or attaining releases of information to facilitate open and coordinated communication can all ease the acceptance of a new provider and facilitate a "warm handoff" that increases the likelihood of service engagement. When refugee and immigrant families have multiple treatment providers and are unsure "who does what," it can be confusing to both family members and providers; whenever possible, it is important to speak directly with other providers to decrease the amount of indirect communication and to ensure that both the network of providers and the family understand the various provider roles.

At other times, and particularly if a family is already burdened with a number of providers or services, the most expedient approach to addressing socioenvironmental problems may be for a clinician to address these stressors within the context of the therapeutic treatment plan. For example, the relatively simple act of helping a family place a call to the office of Temporary Assistance for Needy Families (TANF) and assisting with associated paperwork may fall outside the typical type of work provided by some therapists yet may take less time than facilitating a referral to a case-management agency. Furthermore, providing this direct assistance to the family may also have the tremendous benefit of building trust and engagement with the family. For a child such as Rayhan, this act may also ultimately directly reduce the stress and dysregulation that he experiences in the school cafeteria.

A clinician's decision about when to provide direct case-management support compared with when to refer to other providers will need to be informed by the clinician's capacities, the availability of a referral network, the needs of the family, and the needs and policies of the mental health agency within which a clinician works. Once a determination is made about how a clinician plans to address various client needs, clear communication with a family about the boundaries of service provision are important; a clinician may become the families' "mail reader and phone-call maker," and this is fine if collaboratively determined to be effective by the family and provider. A clinician may delegate some tasks to a case manager and other professionals and clarify the therapist's role as the "talking doctor." What is important is that a family knows (a) that the clinician recognizes and understands the importance of their needs, (b) that their needs will be addressed as best and as efficiently as possible while avoiding setting up false or unrealistic expectations, and (c) who will be doing what.

As can be seen in Table 5.1, interventions for socioenvironmental stressors can range from very informal to formal, and they can build on the strengths of the child, family, and local community. For Rayhan, the clinician facilitated a referral to a local resettlement agency that provided case-management services to aid the family in both the short term (e.g., connection to TANF) and long term (e.g., employment training). She also made a direct call to a food pantry in the area to let them know the family was coming in and provided the family with a printed bus route to get from her office to the food pantry. After obtaining releases of information, the therapist communicated with the school guidance counselor about how the chaos of the cafeteria contributed to Rayhan's dysregulation, and they collaboratively developed a plan for the school counselor to hold a series of "lunch bunch" meetings, where Rayhan and a few other students from various ethnic backgrounds were able to eat in his office. The guidance counselor in this

TABLE 5.1. Interventions to Reduce the Four Core Stressors

Examples of socioecological core stressor	Examples of core stressor interventions	Possible additional resources/referrals as part of core stressor intervention
Resettlement stress • Difficulties finding adequate housing	• Connect family to housing programs and employment training programs • Write letters of support for housing and employment programs	• Refer to refugee resettlement agency or case manager
Isolation stress • Peers pulling a girl's headscarf, making fun of her dress at school (Discrimination)	• Work with school to address immediate issues related to discrimination or bullying	• Refer to school counselor for additional in-school support and attention to school climate
Acculturative stress • Conflicts between children and parents over new and old cultural values	• Offer home-based services to the family	• Refer families to cultural and community programs that provide effective opportunities for children and parents to spend time together

way both reduced the immediate incidence of PTSD-related dysregulation (by offering Rayhan an alternative to the noisy cafeteria) and helped facilitate social connection for Rayhan. These friendships could then also be sources of support as he returned to lunches in the mainstream cafeteria. Finally, Rayhan's PTSD was also formally addressed through psychopharmacology and trauma-focused psychological interventions.

TRAUMA AND MENTAL HEALTH-FOCUSED INTERVENTIONS

Whereas for some refugee or immigrant children successful intervention with socioenvironmental stressors may significantly aid their adjustment, for others focused treatment of PTSD or other mental health problems is needed (Ellis et al., 2013; Fazel et al., 2016). Although evaluations of refugee and immigrant child mental health interventions lag far behind the general evidence-based mental health treatment models, some studies suggest promising models in the treatment of PTSD for youth of refugee and immigrant backgrounds.

Evidence suggests that interventions grounded in cognitive behavior therapy (CBT), including trauma-focused CBT (TF-CBT; Barrett, Moore, & Sonderegger, 2000; Ehntholt, Smith, & Yule, 2005; Fox, Rossetti, Burns, & Popovich, 2005; L. K. Murray, Cohen, Ellis, & Mannarino, 2008) and cognitive behavioral intervention for trauma in schools (CBITS; Kataoka et al., 2003), may be effective with refugee and immigrant children. Both TF-CBT and CBITS have been implemented across diverse ethnocultural groups, with some preliminary evidence demonstrating effectiveness with youth of refugee and immigrant backgrounds.

TRAUMA-FOCUSED COGNITIVE BEHAVIOR THERAPY

A TF-CBT intervention typically includes psychoeducation about trauma and its effects, emotion-regulation skill building, cognitive coping skills, building a trauma narrative, and parent-child sessions in which the child shares his or her trauma narrative with a parent. TF-CBT also explicitly includes engagement strategies focused on exploring a child and family's cultural practices and mourning rituals, and whether, and in what ways, these practices may be influencing distress (Cohen, Mannarino, & Deblinger, 2006). The evidence for TF-CBT's effectiveness with refugee and immigrant youth populations is limited; however, data are promising. Beehler, Birman, and Campbell (2012) conducted a comprehensive school-based intervention program for a diverse population of immigrant youth in which TF-CBT functioned as the primary trauma intervention model. Youth demonstrated significant PTSD symptom reductions as a result of greater cumulative TF-CBT intervention. Ruiz (2016) published promising results using archival data from a mixed sample of urban-living youth (including majority African American and Latinx youth) in which 3 months of TF-CBT led to reductions in trauma symptoms as measured by the Trauma Symptom Checklist for Children. Additionally, in a small but well-designed case series, Unterhitzenberger and colleagues (2015) found TF-CBT to be effective with six unaccompanied refugee adolescents living in Germany across multiple clinical markers, including reductions in symptoms of PTSD. In providing TF-CBT for refugee and immigrant youth, several culturally responsive considerations may help maximize the effectiveness across intervention components.

IMPLEMENTING TF-CBT WITH REFUGEE AND IMMIGRANT YOUTH

TF-CBT engages parents as experts on their children, and in this way also provides an opportunity for a family's culture to help shape the way treatment is implemented. For instance, families may hold culturally ascribed views about whether or not it is appropriate to talk about sex, and with whom these conversation can be had, which may create challenges in working with a sexually abused child; TF-CBT encourages active exploration of familial and cultural perspectives and encourages providers to work within these frameworks (Child Sexual Abuse Task Force and Research & Practice Core, National Child Traumatic Stress Network, 2004).

Sometimes simple framing and language can help make treatment more acceptable and understandable to families. For instance, psychoeducation that normalizes a child's struggles and frames the rationale for treatment in line with the parent's existing goals for the child can be helpful in enhancing the parent's engagement and commitment to treatment. In Table 5.2 we offer an example of how a psychoeducational module about trauma and its downstream effects can be delivered in a way that draws on parents' own experiences and strengths and uses accessible language. The left column provides sample language that a therapist might use when providing psychoeducation about trauma and its effects to a refugee or immigrant parent; the right column provides notes about what is achieved through this language. Such framing can help parents understand how trauma can affect their child and also help elicit empathy for the child by framing their behaviors as a

TABLE 5.2. Sample Psychoeducational Script for Framing of Traumatic Stress Psychoeducation to a Parent of a Refugee or Immigrant Background

Sample psychoeducational script	What this approach achieves
"Think about how your experiences in war and displacement changed you. Your child was likely also changed by his or her experiences of war and displacement."	Clinician helps parent to understand and identify with some of the child's recent behavior as understandable reactions to war and displacement.
"Imagine if you broke your leg because of an accident. Your leg is injured, and you are feeling a lot of pain. For your leg to heal, it will need medicine, care, support, exercise, and time. When a person has been through a lot of hardship and suffering, his or her mind can also become injured. The mind can also feel a lot of pain. The difference between the leg injury and the injury of the mind, however, is that pain in our mind is not visible to most people. The mind (our pain on the inside) can also heal in a way similar to the healing of the leg, through medicine, care, support, exercise, and time."	Defines trauma in tangible, destigmatizing manner and provides hope of healing. Provides a metaphor that can later be referenced when a child is ready for trauma processing (e.g., that sometimes setting a broken bone or cleaning out a wound is painful but necessary for proper healing).
"As an adult, you might have things you do to help you with the pain you feel from war and displacement, for example, praying, talking to other people who have had similar experiences, or remembering good things that make you happy before the bad things that happened. Tell me how you have managed the pain all these years? We want to help your child to learn ways to help with the pain too, and to help his or her brain to heal."	Provides tangible ideas around coping, helps parents relate to the skill-building the child may learn through CBT, and acknowledges cultural strengths and sources of healing.
"Learning these skills often helps kids do better in school and improve their behavior."	Connects back to parent's stated values and goals.

Note. CBT = cognitive behavioral therapy.

product of past trauma exposure rather than as being due to the child's being "bad" or "misbehaving."

Emotion-regulation skills represent a large suite of potential intervention strategies within TF-CBT. Before teaching a specific emotion-regulation skill, consider whether the activity is culturally appropriate, and reflect on cultural norms, values, and beliefs with the child and family. Prior to introducing a new skill, it is often helpful to first ask about common ways in which the child or other people from their cultural group manage stress or deal with upsetting emotions. Specifically, the clinician might consider what common coping strategies are already used by the child and/or other individuals from the child's culture, such as prayer. Before introducing a new skill, explore whether the skill is culturally appropriate or whether there is something about the skill that might be perceived as offensive, illogical, odd, or culturally incongruent. For instance, a visualization that might be relaxing to one client, such as a beach, may be unfamiliar or a reminder of a difficult migration to another. One therapist learned that his Somali client, who had an agricultural background, felt calmed when looking at or visualizing vegetables.

Cognitive coping skills help youth to identify unhelpful, maladaptive thoughts and replace or restructure them with more helpful, adaptive ones. Using traditional cognitive therapy techniques, such as cognitive restructuring and positive self-talk, can be effective with refugee and immigrant youth. Because refugee and immigrant youth often experience stress related to discrimination and may also be living with real fears related to the threat of deportation, clinicians need to be vigilant about not challenging or restructuring thoughts about bias or threat that may, in fact, be true.

COGNITIVE BEHAVIORAL INTERVENTION FOR TRAUMA IN SCHOOLS

If providing school-based services, CBITS may be an especially useful intervention for youth of refugee and immigrant backgrounds. CBITS was developed to be delivered to low-income, trauma-exposed youth in a school setting, and includes both individual- and group-based intervention components that are focused on psychoeducation about trauma, relaxation, social problem solving, cognitive restructuring, and exposure. Multiple intervention studies have demonstrated CBITS's effectiveness for youth of immigrant backgrounds, with multiple studies highlighting positive trauma treatment effects for ethnically Latinx youth (Allison & Ferreira, 2017; Hoover et al., 2018; Ngo et al., 2008). Although the standard components of CBT may all be applicable in working with refugee and immigrant youth, many of the culturally and linguistically responsive strategies discussed throughout this book may shape specific intervention delivery strategies.

NARRATIVE EXPOSURE THERAPY

Another psychological intervention model that has demonstrated promising results with refugee youth is narrative exposure therapy (KidNET;

Neuner et al., 2008; Ruf et al., 2010). Narrative exposure therapy is well suited for refugee populations because many refugee youth have repeated trauma exposures or a history of chronic upheaval (or both) that cannot be adequately captured in a description of discrete trauma episodes, as is commonly conducted in many trauma models (Cohen, Mannarino, & Deblinger, 2017). Although establishing one discrete index trauma that leads to impairment may be helpful for refugee youth, this is often the exception, not the rule. For example, in a community sample of Somali youth resettled in the United States ($n = 144$), children had experienced an average of seven discrete traumatic events, ranging as high as 22 (Ellis, MacDonald, Lincoln, & Cabral, 2008). Narrative exposure therapy addresses the challenge of multiple clinically important traumatic events by facilitating the development of a life narrative (Neuner et al., 2008). Beginning from early childhood, the clinician helps the child place important events, both positive and painful, along a visual timeline. The timeline is then used as an anchor to develop a narrative integrating both hot memories (i.e., sensory information, cognitions, emotions, and physiological feeling) and cold memories (i.e., contexts, facts; Robjant & Fazel, 2010). A lifeline trauma and resilience narrative is developed over multiple sessions and can include physical objects and drawings to help the child understand, visualize, integrate, and externalize their developmental narrative. For example, in practice, on a large piece of paper the clinician and child could make a long line and label different events with stickers depicting stones (e.g., adversities, traumas) and flowers (e.g., positive experiences, moments of resilience). It's important to end this line with a series of concentric circles so as to communicate that the child has an open future and a lot more life to live. Because the nature of refugee experiences often involves shared family trauma, sharing a refugee child's trauma narrative may also mean asking parents to revisit their own trauma histories. Additional support for parents during this time, and a thoughtful assessment of whether the parent is ready to share in the narrative, may be indicated.

Regardless of the approach to trauma processing that a clinician chooses to implement, it is critical that this work occur only after the social environment is sufficiently stable and when the child has the necessary skills to manage potentially intense emotions. This may include, but is not limited to, skills in emotion identification, emotion regulation, cognitive coping (restructuring and defusion), present-moment grounding, and relaxation skills in order for the child to be fully able to engage and benefit from trauma narration. Careful attention to core stressors related to isolation, acculturation, and resettlement can help stabilize the social context so that a child is better able to tolerate and benefit from trauma-focused treatment.

CONSIDERATIONS FOR THE PSYCHOPHARMACOLOGICAL TREATMENT OF REFUGEE CHILDREN

Psychiatric medication is at times indicated to address emotional and behavioral problems in refugee youth. Unfortunately, compared with psychosocial interventions, even less is currently known about evidence-based psychopharmacology for refugees, with no currently available published medication intervention trials with refugee youth. In a 2017 review paper, 15 pharmacological intervention studies with refugee adults were reviewed, but because of limited power and inconsistent study designs, the authors reported that there is not yet evidence for formal psychopharmacological recommendations for treating depression and PTSD in refugee populations (Sonne, Carlsson, Bech, & Mortensen, 2017).

Of the limited available psychopharmacological evidence, Smajkic and colleagues (2001) found significant reductions in PTSD and depression symptom severity, as well as improvements in Global Assessment of Functioning (GAF) scores, following a 6-week treatment with sertraline (a selective serotonin reuptake inhibitor antidepressant) and paroxetine (SSRI, antidepressant) in a trial with adult Bosnian refugees. Another treatment group was treated with venlafaxine (a serotonin-norepinephrine reuptake inhibitor antidepressant) and evidenced significant reductions in PTSD symptom severity and improvements in GAF scores, but had no changes in depression and reported significant side effects. Otto et al. (2003) found that the greatest improvements in a study of Cambodian refugees were those treated with combined sertraline and 10 sessions of CBT. More recently, Sonne and colleagues demonstrated that, in a diverse sample of adult refugee clients (98 on venlafaxine and 109 on sertraline), small but significant pretreatment to posttreatment differences were found on the Harvard Trauma Questionnaire for both medicines; sertraline slightly outperformed venlafaxine on several secondary outcome measures (Sonne, Carlsson, Bech, Elklit, & Mortensen, 2016). On balance, the current psychopharmacology evidence does not clearly point to any broad-based contraindications when prescribing for refugee populations, but some psychiatric leaders believe the likelihood of transformative interventions for refugee populations with psychopharmacological interventions is quite low (Rousseau, 2018).

It is important to note that suggestions related to prescribing psychiatric medication for refugee children may be met with resistance by refugee families. There are times when refugee parents might say they agree to psychiatric treatment out of respect for the provider but, in reality, reject treatment by dropping out of treatment, changing providers, or not following treatment recommendations. Attention to the cultural background of the child and to the meaning that the family ascribes to their child's psychological distress can help to lay the groundwork for a more successful prescriber–client relationship.

Providers who work with refugee communities may feel that they spend significant time trying to convince a caregiver to accept the recommendation for psychopharmacology, unaware that, for refugees from historically collectivistic cultures, an important decision around a child's medical care is often made in consultation with other family members and with the community or religious leaders. Becoming attuned to who else should be "in the room" for such a decision will enhance the likelihood that the most family-responsive and child-focused decisions are made. One simple but powerful recommendation is for parents to bring their family and community members to a meeting with the prescribing clinician—this allows for all parties invested in the decision to be in the room in order to facilitate open and inclusive dialogue.

Cultural attitudes and understanding of psychiatric medications may also affect medication adherence among refugee populations (Lin, Fancher, & Cheung, 2010). Some families of refugee backgrounds may assume that psychiatric medications function similarly to medications such as pain relievers, in that medication should be taken when symptoms are felt and are expected to lead to rapid and immediate symptom relief (Mendenhall, Kelleher, Baird, & Doherty, 2008). This perspective may lead some refugee parents or youth to discontinue their medication if it does not work immediately or as soon as symptoms subside. Ongoing monitoring and education around the reasons why psychiatric medication needs to be taken consistently may improve medication adherence and understanding. Possible barriers to taking medication—including concerns that Western medications are addictive, concerns that religious fasting prohibits taking medication, or preferences for traditional nonpharmaceutical remedies—should be reviewed openly with families, ideally in consultation with cultural or religious experts.

To sum up, although the psychosocial needs of refugee children typically span multiple levels of the social ecology and call for interdisciplinary solutions, an individual clinician can nonetheless provide tremendous support and help by recognizing and seeking to address this range of needs. Treatment may be most effective when it addresses the four core stressors; whether this is done by knitting together existing resources and services or by providing direct assistance, therapists can set in motion integrated care for refugee youth and families. Once socioenvironmental stressors have been attended to, or in tandem with those efforts, therapists may also want to draw on the evidence-based models of trauma-focused treatment described above. Increasingly, multitiered models of intervention that explicitly and pragmatically integrate different services are considered the gold standard for caring for refugee children (Rousseau, 2018; Weine, 2011, 2008). In Chapter 6, we introduce some of these models and the ways in which they can reshape the system of care for refugees.

LIST OF RESOURCES

Trauma-Focused Cognitive Behavioral Therapy (TF-CBT):

These websites provide foundational information on TF-CBT and include resources related to attaining individual certification and implementing TF-CBT across programs and communities.

- https://tfcbt.org
- https://tfcbt2.musc.edu
- https://www.nctsn.org/sites/default/files/resources//how_to_implement_tfcbt.pdf

Cognitive Behavioral Intervention for Trauma in Schools (CBITS)

This website offers free resources to support the implementation of CBITS and provides information about online and in-person training.

- https://cbitsprogram.org

Narrative Exposure Therapy (NET and KidNET)

This website provides information on NET and KidNET, describes the evidence base for each, and highlights ongoing projects around the world. The NET manual is available for purchase.

- https://www.vivo.org/en/

This website provides an overview of NET and case examples to illustrate its use.

- https://www.apa.org/ptsd-guideline/treatments/narrative-exposure-therapy

6 INTEGRATING MENTAL HEALTH CARE INTO SCHOOL OR MEDICAL SETTINGS

Collaborative and Interdisciplinary Models of Care

So far, we have focused on approaches to engaging, assessing, and working with immigrant and refugee children and families that can fit within more traditional models of mental health service delivery. The mental health field, however, is increasingly being shaped by innovative models of care that integrate across service systems (Hodgkinson, Godoy, Beers, & Lewin, 2017; Sanchez et al., 2018). Service systems are shifting toward caring for the whole child and addressing mental health and psychological wellness as an integral component of child health and well-being. For refugee and immigrant children, who commonly contend with stressors and challenges across multiple settings, this is a welcome and necessary shift. How can mental health clinicians build on these integrative models to better serve refugee and immigrant youth and families? In this chapter, we describe how pediatric collaborative-care models and school-based models are particularly well-suited to serving refugee and immigrant youth. We then provide an in-depth look at one specific collaborative model of care: trauma systems therapy for refugees (TST-R).

http://dx.doi.org/10.1037/0000163-006
Mental Health Practice With Immigrant and Refugee Youth: A Socioecological Framework, by B. H. Ellis, S. M. Abdi, and J. P. Winer

PEDIATRIC COLLABORATIVE CARE MODELS: PEDIATRIC INTEGRATED CARE/MEDICAL HOME MODEL

Pediatric and primary care settings offer a logical setting for reaching refugee and immigrant children with mental health needs. For example, all newly arriving refugees receive domestic medical screening as part of the resettlement process (Ellis, Ferris, Shattuck-Heidorn, Kim, & Elmore, 2018). Although mental health screening is not routinely implemented in these visits (Hvass & Wejse, 2017), these initial contacts offer an opportunity to introduce families to mental health care systems and to identify children with particular mental health needs. In the early period after initial resettlement, however, refugee and immigrant families typically need to attend to the many tasks of setting up life in a new country and are less able to focus on their own or their children's mental health care; in addition, some refugee children demonstrate a "honeymoon" period soon after resettlement, and only later do ongoing mental health needs emerge. For these reasons, placing mental health services in the context of a more ongoing medical relationship may make sense. Furthermore, embedding mental health services in primary care can facilitate the destigmatization of mental health services (Arora, Godoy, & Hodgkinson, 2017).

Collaborative care broadly refers to approaches to providing mental health care in an integrated or coordinated manner with physical and behavioral health care providers (Peek & the National Integration Academy Council, 2013). Collaborative care teams frequently are interdisciplinary; in some settings, community health workers integrated within the team function much like cultural brokers, acting as a trusted bridge between patients and providers and contributing additional support and education for families (Brownstein, Hirsch, Rosenthal, & Rush, 2011). Although research on the effectiveness of integrated care for refugees is scant, research into the effectiveness of collaborative care with other low-resource and high-risk populations has been promising (Esala, Vukovich, Hanbury, Kashyap, & Joscelyne, 2018). Collaborative care has also demonstrated success in serving children who have experienced trauma (Schilling, Fortin, & Forkey, 2015). Integrated care may be especially helpful for refugees and immigrants who frequently present with somatic symptoms (Mollica, Poole, Son, Murray, & Tor, 1997) as well as other medical and psychosocial needs. Thus, its application to refugee and immigrant children and its potential to overcome significant hurdles to their engagement in mental health care are promising.

The Refugee Integrated Behavioral Health Care Program at the Lynn Community Health Center in Massachusetts provides one example of an integrated care model reaching refugees. Linked with the region's Refugee Health Assessment Program, in which newly arriving refugees receive initial medical care and screening, the integrated program also provides mental health screening and ongoing medical and behavioral health care (diGrazia, 2018). The program also works with community organizations to support the breadth of needs new refugees face, such as learning English and gaining employment (diGrazia, 2018). Although evaluation data are not available, the program annually serves 200 to 500 refugees (diGrazia, 2018).

SCHOOL-BASED MODELS

Schools offer another logical and pragmatic point of engagement for refugee and immigrant youth and families. Refugee and immigrant families often value education highly and may be more likely to accept mental health services when they are embedded within the school (Tyrer & Fazel, 2014). Mental health services in the school context may also be seen as more trustworthy and may be easily framed as "fostering school success," rather than "treating mental illness," which is more stigmatizing and off-putting for families (Sanchez et al., 2018; Santiago, Raviv, & Jaycox, 2018). School-based services also overcome many of the practical barriers faced in outpatient settings, such as transportation to appointments (Rousseau & Guzder, 2008). Refugee and immigrant students spend a significant portion of their time in the school setting, and direct observations of a child's socioemotional functioning, as well as collateral contact with educational professionals, can be helpful for assessment and initial formulation. Mental health providers embedded in school settings have the advantage of communicating directly with teachers both to understand how the youth is functioning socially and academically and to provide education around the factors that might be driving the youth's behavioral disruptions or inability to concentrate (Fazel, Garcia, & Stein, 2016). In addition, the migrant experience (often including gaps in formal education), as well as mental health problems, can contribute to poor academic functioning (McCloskey & Southwick, 1996; Rousseau, 1995); mental health services can serve to support refugee and immigrant children's academic success. Evaluations of a variety of school-based services suggest that these interventions appeal to refugee youth (Fazel et al., 2016) and effectively reduce their psychological symptoms (Tyrer & Fazel, 2014).

Although school-based services have many advantages related to access and stigma reduction, they may not be sufficient for the needs of all refugee and immigrant children. Engaging parents in treatment and fully understanding how the home context contributes to the child's functioning may be more difficult in a school-based setting (Girio-Herrera & Owens, 2017). In addition, mechanisms for addressing core stressors, many of which fall outside of the school setting, are still essential. Multitiered and multimodal interventions that are based in a school setting offer a means of addressing these concerns (Sullivan & Simonson, 2016; Tyrer & Fazel, 2014). A model developed by Fazel and colleagues (2009) used a team of psychiatrists and art therapists to provide support to students both individually and through recommending classroom interventions. A program implemented in two school districts in New Jersey, Cultural Adjustment and Trauma Services (CATS), provided comprehensive school-based services to first- and second-generation immigrant children experiencing cultural adjustment or trauma-related needs (Beehler, Birman, & Campbell, 2012). Under the CATS model, referred students received services tailored to their specific needs; services included outreach that helped to address resettlement stressors, clinical services such as CBT or TF-CBT, family services, and support in coordinating services (Beehler et al., 2012). Trauma systems therapy for refugees, described in more detail below, is a phase-based multitiered model of care that explicitly addresses socioecological stressors as well as trauma-related mental health problems (Ellis et al., 2013).

TRAUMA SYSTEMS THERAPY FOR REFUGEES

TST-R is an adaptation of the model trauma systems therapy (Saxe, Ellis, & Kaplow, 2007; Saxe et al., 2015) for the specific needs of refugees and immigrant youth and families. Originally adapted for and implemented with Somali students at a middle school in Boston, Massachusetts, the model has since been implemented with diverse ages (elementary through high school) and cultural groups, including Bhutanese (Adhikari, Benson, Nisewaner, & Abdi, 2013; Cardeli et al., 2019).

TST-R provides a model for how multitiered, phase-based services that are based in a school setting can leverage the benefits and infrastructure of an already trusted setting (e.g., school) while also having broad reach into the community and caregiving systems when indicated. TST-R draws on a public health framework to offer different levels of service depending on need; although the broadest level of the program, Tier 1, is indicated for whole communities, higher tiers of service are progressively more focused. Each of the four tiers of service is described in more detail below. (See Figure 6.1.)

FIGURE 6.1. TST-R: Multitiered Model for Engaging Communities, Youth, and Families in Services

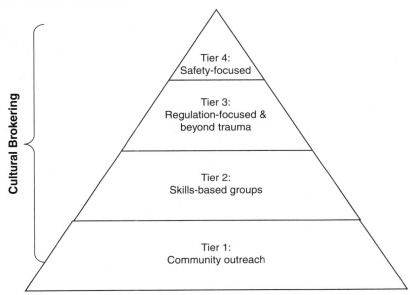

Tier 1: Community Outreach

Without engagement, the most elegantly designed intervention program is simply a hollow concept on paper. A program has no value unless the community and clients it is trying to serve perceive value; the time, effort, and trust involved in allowing a child to participate in treatment will only be put forth if families believe it meets their needs in a manner that is not in conflict with their culture. Often, families look to community leaders to guide their actions, so building trust and partnership with these individuals is key to engagement.

Within TST-R, Tier 1 services seek to build this community-level engagement. Tier 1 services typically involve ongoing community outreach, engagement, and education with both community members and leaders and with service providers and systems. Outreach can be conducted by both clinicians and cultural brokers with the goal of coeducation and colearning related to cultural values and norms, expectations held by the service system, expectations held by the community, and mental health. This outreach is not simply "spreading the word" about a program, but rather deeply engaging community members in ongoing discussions about perceived needs and values and how the program can best fit and address the needs of the community.

Outreach to mental health and service system providers works to share the learned information about community needs and cultural norms, and it contributes to building cultural responsivity. Collectively, these outreach activities increase acceptance and engagement of services, decrease stigma and confusion about mental health services, and enhance cultural relevance of the program by integrating community knowledge, beliefs, and feedback into service delivery. Activities can include both traditional forms of outreach, such as a booth with flyers at a community event, and creative community-engagement processes that bring people together and allow opportunities for cultural integration and affirmation, such as organizing a youth soccer team or an after-school gardening group. Having members of a program team participate in nonstigmatized activities that allow for relationship building facilitates later trust and engagement in settings or relationships that may be less comfortable and familiar to families, such as mental health services. Community engagement, outreach, learning, and education remain a core set of activities throughout the duration of a program; sustained outreach allows the program to respond more nimbly to changing concerns in the community, retains trust and engagement, and offers opportunities for iterative adaptation of the program to best fit the culture and community it seeks to serve. (See Table 6.1.)

The following case example illustrates how Tier 1 services can lay an essential foundation for a trusting partnership between refugee communities

TABLE 6.1. TST-R Tier 1: Community Engagement

Example activities and processes	Candidate mechanisms (i.e., why we think it works)	Expected outcomes
• School-wide training on refugee mental health and cultural humility • Community meetings generating discussion of perceptions of youth needs • Establishing a community advisory board	• Colearning between school/providers/community related to mental health, the refugee experience, and culture • Shared vision, sense of trust, and equitable partnership • Community input and buy-in	• High levels of engagement of refugee youth in services • More culturally relevant services and enhanced cultural knowledge of service providers • Trauma- and refugee-informed social service systems • Enhanced well-being and sense of efficacy of refugee community members, educators, and mental health providers

and providers. Although community outreach is a central component of TST-R, it is not unique to TST-R; the basic principles of Tier 1 can be applied in the context of the development of any refugee and immigrant-focused mental health program.

A clinical service provider was considering applying for grant funding to support a program implementing TST-R with Somali refugee youth. To find out whether the program resonated with community members, she asked a coworker, who was herself Somali, to organize a meeting with a diverse group of community gatekeepers to discuss how they could support the refugee community. When they sat down with a group of religious and community leaders as part of Tier 1 work, the clinician and her coworker thanked the leaders for meeting them, and then the clinician asked the leaders if they could tell her about the community and the work they did within it. The head religious leader spent an hour talking about the struggles of refugee families, about how much of his work was about trying to help families who struggled with an acculturation gap between parents and children, and about children who struggled with substance abuse and behavior problems. When he finished, the clinician said, "I am in awe of the amount of work that you and other community members are doing to help children and families in your community. I can learn so much from you. Will you help me understand what the youth in your community need, and how I can perhaps add to the amazing work you do to support them? The goals you shared are the very ones that I have: helping children succeed, reducing family conflict and violence, and helping this community do well by addressing issues that are related to experiences of war and loss. We have the same goals but different tools to use; my work could never replace yours, and in fact my work could never succeed without people like you and my coworker helping me understand and reach the community. I am hoping we can work together to solve these problems."

By taking an approach that is deeply informed by cultural humility and respect for community strengths and existing community resources, the clinician was able to develop a collaborative relationship with community leaders. Often, people in refugee and immigrant communities go to religious leaders or trusted community leaders for issues related to mental illness. By developing this respectful and collaborative relationship, this clinician was able to engage powerful gatekeepers in the community as partners rather than competitors, thus building trust with other community members who follow these opinion leaders.

Tier 2: Skills-Based Groups

Once a community is sufficiently engaged, more active prevention and intervention activities can begin. In TST-R, Tier 2 services provide universal services for refugee and immigrant youth within a school setting through skills-based groups. The primary goal of these skills-based groups is to help youth build cognitive, behavioral, interpersonal, and emotion-regulation skills to effectively manage stressors common to the refugee and immigrant youth experience (e.g., acculturative and isolation stress). For many refugee and immigrant students, the opportunity to gather with other students with a shared background can also foster a sense of belonging, connection, validation, and trust within the school setting. Cofacilitated by a mental health clinician and a cultural broker, group leaders model cross-cultural communication and collaboration and serve as points of connection and coordination among teachers, community leaders, and broader systems. The groups also provide an opportunity to strengthen a sense of trust and connection between providers and students and their families in relation to a nonstigmatizing group. If group leaders observe mental health concerns among students in the group, including problems associated with traumatic stress, the foundational relationship is already in place with families to help facilitate acceptance of a referral to further mental health services (Tiers 3 and 4 of the TST-R program). (See Table 6.2.)

The TST-R group curriculum, which has been adapted for different ethnic groups (Abdi & Nisewaner, 2009; Adhikari et al., 2013) and for youth of various ages (Winer, Issa, Park, Nisewaner, & Abdi, 2018), is composed of three broad modules: (a) building rapport and establishing community guidelines, (b) managing acculturative stressors and teaching effective communication strategies, and (c) emotion identification and regulation

TABLE 6.2. TST-R Tier 2: Skills-Based Groups

Example activities and processes	Candidate mechanisms (i.e., why we think it works)	Expected outcomes
• Manual-based group interventions (8–12 sessions) • Co-led by a clinician and cultural broker whose ethnicity matches youth served in the group • Embedded within a school or trusted community system	• Skills-focused, so youth can learn and practice practical strategies to improve emotion regulation and conflict resolution • Models effective and supportive cross-cultural communication, collaboration, and trust • Offers psychosocial support in a nonstigmatized, validating, and easily accessible setting.	• Increased sense of social belongingness • Decreased symptoms of isolation and mental health problems • Enhanced interpersonal skills to manage conflict • Enhanced emotion regulation skills • Decreased stigma toward psychological services and mental health providers

skills. Adolescent groups include additional sessions on sociocultural identity development and goal and value identification as youth begin to engage in more future-oriented thinking while simultaneously being confronted with discrimination and bias in their everyday lives (Winer et al., 2018). Although content from the four core stressors is woven throughout the intervention, Tier 2 groups primarily target strategies for managing isolation and acculturative stress. For youth for whom resettlement stressors continue to pose functional distress and impairment, group leaders offer referrals to appropriate social services.

The following is a case example of a Bhutanese adolescent who attended TST-R Tier 2 groups:

> Meena, a young Bhutanese teenager, was struggling at both home and school. She was skipping school and staying out late. Meena spoke English well. Since moving to the United States, she had adopted a number of behaviors that she had observed among some of her American peers, such as smoking and drinking, skipping school, and disobeying parents. She also began dating a boy from a lower caste, a flagrant violation of family and cultural expectations. Parents of other Bhutanese teenagers in the community would not let Meena associate with their children for fear of her being a bad influence. The school counselor tried several times to get her help, but the parents refused treatment for their daughter. When a TST-R program was implemented in Meena's school, a Bhutanese cultural broker was able to communicate with Meena's parents in their native language about the potential value of Meena's attendance at a TST-R group. The cultural broker also highlighted that all Bhutanese youth at the school were invited to participate, not just those who were struggling, and the parents readily consented to Meena's participation.
>
> In the group, Meena quickly developed a strong attachment to the cultural broker, who provided a model of how someone could be successful within American culture while also maintaining elements of her Bhutanese culture. In addition, Meena was able to interact with other teens from her community. Meena started hanging out with other kids from the Bhutanese community outside of the group and began to reintegrate with her community. Importantly, the cultural broker and clinician were able to initiate a referral for home-based services to help reduce acculturative conflict between Meena and her parents and to provide resources to address resettlement stressors that were adding to home tension, such as parental unemployment.

As the case illustrates, Tier 2 skills-based groups serve multiple functions. They help provide foundational cognitive, behavioral, interpersonal, and emotion-regulation skill building for youth who are struggling with family and peer relationships; they can address isolation stress by connecting youth to peer and community support; and they can act as a gateway to higher levels of care for youth who need them.

Tiers 3 and 4: Trauma Systems Therapy

Often youth who are receiving Tier 2 services but who are in need of more focused mental health treatment are referred for treatment based on the TST model (Saxe, Ellis, & Brown, 2015). TST treatment is an organizational model for integrating different services, as well as a clinical model that orients these services around specific treatment targets. The goal of TST is to address what is referred to in the treatment model as the *trauma system*: (a) a child who is experiencing trauma-related emotional dysregulation (or *survival states*), and (b) a social environment or system of care (or both) that is not sufficiently able to manage or prevent this dysregulation (Saxe et al., 2015). Within TST, a clinician seeks to understand how specific stimuli or stressors in the social environment relate to episodes of dysregulation, or survival states. These patterns of stimuli and responses become the focus of treatment; providers then draw on an array of interventions guided by treatment phase both to stabilize the social environment and to increase a child's capacity to self-regulate. For refugee and immigrant children, addressing the four core stressors is often a critical component of stabilizing the social environment. Treatment is provided by a dyadic team of a clinician and cultural broker; at times other providers, including case managers, psychiatrists, or legal advocates, may be integrated into the treatment team.

As detailed in the TST manual (Saxe et al., 2015), TST consists of three phases of treatment: safety-focused treatment, regulation-focused treatment, and beyond trauma treatment. Assessment of both (a) the degree of a child's dysregulation and (b) the stability of the social environment determine in which phase of treatment a child starts. Children assessed to be experiencing high levels of dysregulation or less stable social environments receive more intensive services (Tier 4). Below we describe the three TST treatment phases, starting with the most intensive level of intervention: Tier 4, safety-focused treatment. More detailed information about the treatment model is available in the book *Trauma Systems Therapy for Children and Teens* (Saxe et al., 2015; see Figure 6.2 and Table 6.3).

Tier 4: Safety-Focused Treatment

Safety-focused treatment is the most intensive level of care delivered in TST-R. This phase of treatment is appropriate when a child is living in a threatening or harmful social environment or when the child is exhibiting dangerous behavior, or both. For example, safety-focused treatment would be indicated for a child who is experiencing abuse or neglect at home, or is physically assaultive, self-harming, or using substances. This phase of

FIGURE 6.2. TST Grid Used to Determine Phase of Treatment and Specific Intervention Targets and Goals

		Social environmental stability		
		Stable	**Distressed**	**Threatening**
Child's survival states	**No survival states**	Beyond trauma	Beyond trauma	Safety-focused
	Survival states	Regulation-focused	Regulation-focused	Safety-focused
	Dangerous survival states	Regulation-focused	Safety-focused	Safety-focused

Two dimensions are assessed under TST/TST-R: the degree to which the child experiences survival states (e.g., emotional dysregulation), and the degree to which the social environment is able to help and protect the child from those survival states and the stressors that drive them. Based on the assessment of each of these dimensions, the phase of treatment is determined: safety-focused, regulation-focused, or beyond trauma.

treatment is dedicated to stabilizing a child's social environment so that it is no longer harmful and so that caregivers can reduce the child's vulnerability to shifting into dangerous survival states. A child's immediate safety is the first priority. If the social environment is assessed as "dangerous," the primary goal is to address the socioenvironmental threat immediately or to move the child to a safer environment. If the child is demonstrating dangerous behaviors, the primary goal is to diminish dysregulation immediately through reducing stressors that trigger the dysregulation or through psychopharmacology so that the child can be maintained in a home setting. Sometimes both sets of activities are needed to establish safety.

Safety-focused treatment interventions are delivered within the home setting; the clinician and the cultural broker are partners both in providing mental health services and in addressing stressors in the social environment that may be contributing to the child's dysregulation. Addressing the four

TABLE 6.3. Categorization of Child's Survival States and Social Environment States

Child's survival states	Definitions
No survival states	1. Does not display episodes of survival-in-the-moment (shifts in *Awareness*, *Affect*, and *Action*) when a threat is perceived in the present environment.
	2. If the child displays shifts in awareness, affect, and action when a threat is perceived, neither the episode itself, nor the anticipation of such episodes, results in any problem with the child's functioning.
Survival states	1. Displays episodes of survival-in-the-moment (shifts in *Awareness*, *Affect*, and *Action*) when threat is perceived in the present environment.
	2. The shift in *Action* during such episodes does not include potentially dangerous behaviors (e.g., self-destructive, aggressive, substance-abusing, risky eating or sexual behaviors).
	3. Such episodes, or their anticipation, result in problems with the child's functioning.
Dangerous survival states	1. Displays episodes of survival-in-the-moment (shifts in *Awareness*, *Affect*, and *Action*) when threat is perceived in the present environment.
	2. The shift in *Action* during such episodes includes potentially dangerous behaviors (e.g., self-destructive, aggressive, substance-abusing, risky eating or sexual behaviors).
	3. Such episodes, or their anticipation, result in problems with the child's functioning.

The social environment	Definitions
Stable	1. The child's immediate caregivers are able to *help* with the child's vulnerability to switching into survival states and to *protect* him/her from perceived and actual threats, including Core Stressors that might be impacting the family in resettlement; OR
	2. Other adults in the child's life are able to *help* with the child's vulnerability to switching into survival states and to *protect* the child; OR
	3. The child's service system has been accessed and, if the child's immediate family or extended social network is unable to *help* with the child's vulnerability to switching into survival states or to *protect* him/her from environmental threats, services are in place that effectively provide these functions

TABLE 6.3. Categorization of Child's Survival States and Social Environment States (*Continued*)

The social environment	Definitions
Distressed	1. The child's immediate caregivers are unable to adequately *help* with the child's vulnerability to switching into survival states and/or to *protect* him/her from perceived threats; AND
	2. Other adults in the child's life are unable to adequately *help* with the child's vulnerability to switching into survival states and/or to *protect* the child from perceived threats; AND
	3. The child's service system is not able to effectively *help* with the child's vulnerability to switching to survival states and/or to *protect* the child from perceived threats.
Threatening	1. The child's immediate caregivers are unable to adequately *help* with the child's vulnerability to switching into survival states and/or to *protect* him/her from actual threats; AND
	2. Other adults in the child's life are unable to adequately *help* with the child's vulnerability to switching into survival states and/or to *protect* the child from actual threats; AND
	3. The child's service system is not able to effectively *help* with the child's vulnerability to switching to survival states and/or to *protect* the child from actual threats.

core stressors often forms a critical part of the work. Given the more intense needs of the child and family, the clinician–cultural broker dyad will typically meet with a family twice a week or more. Individual sessions with the child may also take place at school or in an office. (See Table 6.4.)

The cultural broker plays a particularly important role in the safety-focused phase of treatment. Specifically, cultural brokers are carriers of important cultural information related to parenting practices, traditional customs, and family roles, and they can support the clinician in navigating these cross-cultural complexities. In addition, cultural brokers can provide important information to the family about treatment, thereby addressing their fears related to social services, mental health, or hospital systems. While establishing safety the TST-R team may also need to engage in advocacy. This can include calling a supervisor within the child welfare system, talking to providers in an inpatient unit, or helping a parent find safer housing.

Safety-Focused Treatment has three related components:

- Prioritize and establish safety
  - Activities that will ensure the environment becomes safe in a time frame that is appropriate for the level of risk or that gets the child to a safe environment if needed.

TABLE 6.4. TST-R Tier 4: Stabilizing the Social Environment

Example activities and processes	Candidate mechanisms (i.e., why we think it works)	Expected outcomes
• Home-based care 2-3 times/week by a clinician–cultural broker dyad to support parents in implementing effective parenting strategies • Referrals to additional services or means of accessing benefits to address core stressors such as food scarcity	• Intensive community-based work allows for thorough assessment of socioenvironmental needs and appropriate interventions/resources to address them • Home-based care decreases practical barriers to engagement such as transportation • Pairing of cultural broker with clinician enhances engagement and trust with families	• Decreases in home and family stress • Decreases in acculturative and resettlement stressors • Decreases in risky behavioral dysregulation

- Reduce survival states and maintain safety

  – Activities that support the continuation of safety, including addressing Four Core Stressors.

- Caring for caregivers

  – Activities that support caregivers, including supporting refugee and immigrant parents in learning strategies for parenting in a new cultural context.

To illustrate, we return to Meena, the Bhutanese adolescent enrolled in Tier 2 TST-R groups:

After a few weeks of listening to Meena, in the groups, continually reference distress and conflict at home, the group leaders determined that Meena needed more intensive services. The group leaders had developed a trusting relationship with Meena's parents through their previous meetings related to enrolling Meena in the group; when the cultural broker met again with the family to suggest that Meena could benefit from additional support through a clinician–cultural broker team with the TST-R program, the parents readily consented. As the TST-R clinician conducted the evaluation, she observed that the degree of distress and conflict in the family was significant and likely driving some of Meena's dangerous behaviors, such as her substance use and staying out late. In particular, she learned that the father sometimes became extremely angry and that Meena would respond by running out of the house and not returning for hours. The clinician assessed Meena to be in the safety-focused phase of treatment and recommended home-based services to help address some of the critical socioecological stressors. The home-based team included a new clinician and the cultural broker that Meena and her family already respected and trusted. After meeting with Meena and her family, the team identified multiple stressors, including resettlement (parental unemployment), acculturative (parent–child acculturation gap), past trauma (war and domestic violence), and isolation (parental lack of social support). Identifying that parental unemployment was contributing to significant stress in the family and often triggered her father's rage and Meena's subsequent dangerous behavior, the team immediately focused on helping engage the father in an employment training program. They simultaneously worked with Meena to build her self-regulation skills so that she had alternative strategies to manage her intense emotions when her father was upset. A few months later, Meena came to group smiling and mentioned that she was heading home early as their family was having a celebratory dinner in honor of her father's new job. Over the next couple of months, the home-based team observed significantly reduced levels of stress in the family, and Meena began to voluntarily stay at home some weekend nights to spend more time with her parents.

With the social environmental stressors significantly reduced, Meena no longer demonstrated the same dangerous behavior as before. Although she continued to have screaming matches with her parents and often withdrew into her room, she no longer stayed out late and had stopped experimenting with substances. Within the TST-R program, the team shifted her to Tier-3, regulation-focused treatment. Not all refugee and immigrant children will need to begin in safety-focused treatment; for those who do not, or for those like Meena who graduate from safety-focused treatment, TST-R Tier 3 is appropriate.

Tier 3: Regulation-Focused Treatment and Beyond Trauma Treatment

Tier 3 of TST-R encompasses two separate phases of treatment—regulation-focused and beyond trauma. These phases are grouped together in Tier 3 because the services team—typically an outpatient-based clinician and cultural broker team—remains the same across these phases of treatment. Typically, Tier 3 services are initiated when a child's survival states are more regulated (episodes of dysregulation are not dangerous in nature) and the social environment is either stable or distressed but not threatening. As a child progresses through Tier 3 treatment and becomes increasingly capable of managing emotions he or she moves from regulation-focused to beyond trauma treatment. (See Table 6.5.)

Regulation-focused treatment is appropriate when a child demonstrates some degree of emotion dysregulation and may or may not also be experiencing significant stress (but not danger) in the social environment. For example, a child who regularly screams or shuts down when around rowdy peers at school might benefit from regulation-focused treatment.

TABLE 6.5. TST-R Tier 3: Emotion Regulation and Trauma Processing

Example activities and processes	Candidate mechanisms (i.e., why we think it works)	Expected outcomes
• Outpatient-based emotion regulation skill-building using a structured Managing Emotions Guide • Trauma processing through narrative development	• Clinician helps child and family learn from recent concrete examples of child's dysregulation to understand emotional triggers, emotional responses, and effective coping strategies • Child and family learn concrete coping skills • Trauma processing diminishes affective arousal in relation to trauma	• Increased awareness of triggers and signs of dysregulation • Increased use of effective coping and emotion regulation skills • Decreased symptoms of posttraumatic stress disorder, depression, or other trauma-related dysregulation

Primary activities of regulation-focused treatment include:

- building the child's skills to manage environmental signals experienced as threatening ("triggers"),

- teaching emotion identification and cognitive and emotion-regulation skills, and

- consulting with caregivers around parenting and reducing stressors or triggers, as needed, with cultural broker support.

A child and family are ready for the beyond trauma phase of treatment when the social environment is not threatening and the child is generally able to effectively regulate emotions and behaviors when confronted with mild stressors. The primary goals of beyond trauma treatment are to help the child and family move beyond the trauma so that these experiences do not define the child's sense of self and relationships or how others view and treat the child. The primary goals of beyond trauma treatment are captured in the mnemonic STRONG: Strengthening cognitive skills, Telling your story, Reevaluating needs, Orienting to the future, Nurturing parent-child relations, and Going forward. Much of the description in Chapter 5 related to trauma processing with refugees and immigrants is relevant to this phase of treatment.

As can be seen in the case example of Meena, the focus of her treatment shifted as she became increasingly better at regulating her emotions:

Meena's treatment progressed, Meena became much more adept at noticing when she was beginning to, in her words, "flame up." She started talking about how she felt a sinking feeling in her stomach and a flare of anger when her father started to yell at her to behave in certain ways, and how her thoughts went to "Why should I act Bhutanese—look what being Bhutanese has gotten us." She began to try new strategies for managing these feelings when she noticed them and found that praying in her room allowed her to calm down quickly and to be able to rejoin the family. Her father was surprised to learn she was praying and suggested that sometimes the two of them could pray together. As Meena began to develop a life narrative describing what she and her family went through in the refugee camp, she began to describe the sense of despair she had seen in her father's face when they finally came to the United States and he still couldn't provide for his family. She described her anger at all her father had been through and talked about how in some ways she felt like rejecting parts of Bhutanese culture was a way of rejecting the terrible past they had lived through. With her therapist's encouragement, she began trying out different perspectives: Instead of thinking "look what being Bhutanese has gotten us," she tried thinking "look what the war and conflict did to us—it tried to destroy my family, but it can't. Our family and our culture can be stronger than the hatred that got us here." She talked with her therapist about her evolving bicultural identity, and they worked together to help her articulate the values, beliefs, and ideas she held from both Bhutanese and American cultures— shifting from "either or" to "both and." Over time, she found herself in fewer and fewer conflicts with her parents and began to feel a sense of pride in how her family had survived and adapted.

Across all tiers of treatment, TST-R incorporates cultural brokers as central members of the treatment team. Cultural brokers engage in community outreach, colead Tier 2 groups, and partner with clinicians in Tiers 3 and 4 to facilitate engagement and inclusion of family in treatment. They may also provide critical supportive services related to core stressors.

An evaluation of TST-R with Somali refugee students demonstrated high levels of treatment engagement, successful mapping of different tiers of service to different levels of need, reduction in family and daily stressors, and overall effectiveness in reducing mental health symptoms (Ellis et al., 2013). Students receiving TST-R were assessed at baseline, 6 months, and 12 months post–program initiation. At baseline, students referred to Tiers 3 and 4 showed higher levels of PTSD symptoms than those who received Tier 2 only, suggesting that the group leaders and teachers successfully identified students with higher levels of mental health needs. All students who received any element of TST-R demonstrated improvements in mental health symptoms over the course of 6 months. Students who received more intensive services (Tiers 3 and 4) showed continued improvements, and by 12 months post–treatment initiation symptom levels of those students who had been referred for intensive services were indistinguishable from those who had never needed or been referred to more intensive treatment

(Ellis et al., 2013). A separate study evaluated Tier 2 TST-R groups implemented with Bhutanese refugees in Springfield, Massachusetts (Cardeli et al., 2019). Thirty-five Bhutanese students at a middle school received TST-R Tier 2 group interventions; at baseline approximately half of the students had significant PTSD symptomatology. Over the course of the 12-week group intervention students showed a significant decline in PTSD avoidance symptoms; those students who initially met criteria for full or partial PTSD showed particularly steep declines in both PTSD and depression symptoms.

Embedding services within existing service systems, such as primary care settings or schools, has many advantages. This includes greater service integration in order to more comprehensively address barriers to care for refugee and immigrant children and families. Across all of these efforts, however, attention to how the organizational system attends to culture is critical. Fundamentally, services that are built out of genuine partnerships with communities can begin to build the trust and understanding necessary for effective care. Culturally and linguistically responsive practices must be central to services, and attention to the full range of sociocultural stressors that affect refugee and immigrant youth and families is critical.

LIST OF RESOURCES

TST Book: *Trauma Systems Therapy for Children and Teens* (Saxe, Ellis, & Brown, 2015) describes TST, the original model that was adapted for TST-R and that remains the core of TST-R Tiers 3 and 4. The book provides a detailed description of the theoretical underpinnings and practical organization and clinical implementation of TST. Available from major book sellers.

TST-R brief introductory video: (https://tinyurl.com/traumasystems therapy). This 5-minute video provides an overview of the initial Boston-based TST-R program with Somali refugees, Project SHIFA.

Key articles and chapters describing TST-R: These publications review the mental health needs of refugee children and families and discuss the theory and evidence supporting the effectiveness of TST-R at overcoming barriers to providing mental health services to address those needs.

- Benson, M. A., Abdi, S. M., Miller, A. B., & Ellis, B. H. (2019). Trauma systems therapy for refugee children and families. In N. Morina & A. Nickerson (Eds.), *Mental health of refugee and conflict-affected populations: Theory, research, and clinical practice* (pp. 243–260). Cham, Switzerland: Springer.

• Ellis, B. H., Miller, A. B., Abdi, S., Barrett, C., Blood, E. A., & Betancourt, T. S. (2013). Multi-tier mental health program for refugee youth. *Journal of Consulting and Clinical Psychology, 81*, 129–40.

TST-R Training information: Training on the full TST-R model is typically provided to specific organizations intending to implement the model. For more information, contact rtrc@childrens.harvard.edu by e-mail.

7 REFUGEES IN OUR COMMUNITIES

Promoting Whole Community Resilience

Amira is a Syrian refugee and a senior at the local public high school, where she is active in the drama and journalism clubs. Her family is very proud that she recently got a lead role in the school play, and although the family was at first reluctant to allow her to take a role that involved her staying out late to rehearse, appearing in public with male co-actors, and dressing in Western attire, they ultimately agreed that it was an important activity for Amira and so supported her in doing it. Amira also is very involved in the family's local mosque, where she is part of a youth leadership group. Her youth group recently received permission from the mosque leadership to hold an event called "Fighting Hate With Friendship" that would invite youth of all backgrounds to attend and share experiences. The journalism club, which meets in a room decorated with pictures of youth from a range of religious and ethnic groups, has suggested it should run a notice in the school newspaper about the event. Several of the cast members from the play have told Amira they want to attend. The local police offered a security detail outside the mosque to ensure the safety of all participants; on the evening of the event, the officer greets Amira by name and gives her a thumbs up for the work she is doing. Amira smiles back, feeling proud of her communities—her Syrian and Muslim community, her American friends, and the fabric of society that supports them.

http://dx.doi.org/10.1037/0000163-007
Mental Health Practice With Immigrant and Refugee Youth: A Socioecological Framework,
by B. H. Ellis, S. M. Abdi, and J. P. Winer

The story of Amira is one of a well-adjusted, thriving individual, as well as of a resilient community. As Amira moves through her day, she passes through experiences that strengthen her sense of connection to ethnic and religious identity (e.g., her family, her mosque), connect her to the broader community (e.g., school, drama, journalism club), and offer positive ties to the system of government or other authorities that weave through society (e.g., law enforcement, mosque leadership). These three types of social connection—social bonding, social bridging, and social linking, respectively—build resilient communities (Poortinga, 2012). Resilient communities are less likely to experience certain types of adversity, such as violence, and are better prepared to weather such adversity should it occur (Walsh, 2007). For refugees or immigrants who join new communities as a result of extreme adversity, resilient communities that offer diverse, strong social connection can create nurturing and healing environments.

The United States was founded on principles of equality and inclusion. Refugees, by definition, have fled their countries because of persecution related to who they are and what they believe. Although resettlement in the United States provides shelter from such persecution, our communities do not always protect against corrosive experiences of discrimination, exclusion, and marginalization. Racism, religious discrimination, and anti-immigrant sentiments persist. Less overt or unconscious forms of exclusion or bias, including experiences of implicit bias, stereotype threat, and micro-aggressions (brief and commonplace verbal, behavioral, and attitudinal indignities), are prevalent in many refugee and immigrant children's daily experiences (Banaji & Greenwald, 2013; Steele, 1997, 2010; Sue et al., 2007). Imagine an alternative story about Amira that could easily have been true:

> Amira is a Syrian refugee and senior at the local public high school, where she is active in the drama and journalism clubs. She recently tried out for the lead role in a high school play and was cast as a minor character—although she was happy to be in the play, she wondered whether the fact that she wore a headscarf to auditions cost her a lead role. When she confided this concern to a friend, her friend's response was to say, "That is so wrong—you're not like most Muslim girls, you're really outgoing and confident!" She used to be a part of her youth group at the mosque but quit after she was told by another girl that she was "not Muslim enough." The journalism club, which meets in a room decorated with pictures of famous White journalists, suggested they run a commemorative article about 9–11. Amira submitted an article on how she felt about this event as an American. The editor sent the article back asking Amira if she could write "the Muslim perspective" on the incident instead. As she was walking home from school that day, a man yelled, "Go back to your country!" A local police officer who was on the corner looked up and registered the

comment, then looked away. Amira put her head down and continued on her way, wondering where her home really is and where she belongs.

The world Amira travels through in this second story is fraught with messages, overt and covert, of exclusion, stigma, and stereotype. Even a well-intentioned friend conveyed disparaging prejudices through an interpersonal microaggression. Decades of research document the corrosive effect that discrimination has on health, including mental health (Kim & Williams, 2012; Steele, 2010). How can mental health providers work to build more resilient communities? In part, by working to support and strengthen social bonds, bridging, and linking for youth like Amira.

Over the years, there has been much debate about whether societies should become "melting pots" where ethnic identities fade away into a larger societal soup, or "chef salads" where specific characteristics of ethnic groups remain distinct and intact, side by side (American Psychological Association [APA] Presidential Task Force on Immigration, 2012). Ultimately, there is no right or wrong way for an individual to acculturate to a new country. Acculturation has many facets, such as cultural practice, cultural values, and cultural identifications; a given individual may show different patterns of acculturation across these dimensions (Schwartz, Unger, Zamboanga, & Szapocznik, 2010). Recent theory and research have also emphasized the importance of understanding the *context of reception*—that is, the attitudes and expectations that are held within the receiving society related to a particular immigrant group and their acculturation process (Schwartz et al., 2010).

BUILDING COMMUNITY RESILIENCE: THE CLINICIAN'S ROLE

A clinician's job is not to advocate for a specific type of acculturation but to help create conditions that allow refugee or immigrant youth to explore and embrace aspects of his or her identity that feel true, affirming, and in line with his or her goals and values. Below, we provide specific guidance on ways this can be accomplished.

Social Bonds: Strengthening Sense of Connection and Pride in Ethnic Identity

Clinicians can signal respect for a youth's ethnic or religious identity through personal interactions, therapeutic activities, and attention to the physical environment. Taking the time to self-educate about a client's culture of origin communicates that a therapist values that way of being and those experiences. This education should encompass not only the sociopolitical disruption and upheaval that lead to forced migration but also the strengths and beauty of the culture that go far beyond those experiences. Cultures contain within them sources of strength and healing; for instance, the Latinx cultural value of *familism* is associated with better psychological health and has even been found to mitigate the negative effect of migration-related stress (Torres & Santiago, 2018).

Although it is important not to expect clients to become the authority and teacher on the subject of their culture of origin, asking for clients and their family to share about beloved traditions or cultural values can be a way to emphasize the strengths and positives while also communicating interest. It will also help the clinician to understand the values and beliefs that underlie the client's understanding and attitude toward mental health problems and might provide insight into how best to frame the support being provided. Some families may not yet have found ways to practice their traditions, or even their religion, in resettlement, so asking about this and working with the child and family to find a way for families to engage in these valued practices can be an important part of the treatment plan. Because questions of religious practice can sometimes be sensitive and uncomfortable when discussed cross-culturally, it might be helpful for the clinician to frame them in the practice of self-care. The clinician might ask clients what they did before migration when they were experiencing psychological distress. If prayer is identified as one of these helpful and healing activities, the clinician can explore with the clients whether they are still able to engage in this activity and if there are barriers that make spiritual practice difficult.

In one example, a group of Bhutanese refugees that resettled in one neighborhood did not have a place of worship (L. Mulder, personal communication, October 31, 2018). This was causing great distress to the community. The lack of a place to practice their religion was especially painful for the older members of the community, who felt deprived of those fundamental activities and who also worried that the younger generation was losing connection to its religion and culture. Providers and ethnic-based organizations in the area worked together and were able to secure a space for the community to meet and hold religious ceremonies. This generous act not only relieved the community's concerns about not being able to gather for religious practice, but also helped connect and build trust between the refugee community and the wider community.

Youth who are struggling with their identity and families faced with acculturative stress might benefit from connections to coethnics in their community (Jasinskaja-Lahti, Liebkind, Jaakkola, & Reuter, 2006; Noh & Kaspar, 2003; Schweitzer, Melville, Steel, & Lacherez, 2006). Therefore, if a child and family express interest in connecting with their local ethnic group but have not yet done so, therapists can help by exploring local ethnic-based community organizations and the various youth groups or community activities that they support. This could help reduce isolation and provide the family with resources that might support their psychological well-being.

Clinicians can also convey respect for ethnic identity through attention to the physical space. Clinicians may perform a visual scan of their office or workspace: Do the art, books, and toys affirm the value of diverse social and cultural identities? What about the lobby and registration area? Are resources available in multiple languages? Simple changes to the physical environment can subtly signal to youth and families that, at least in the context of this office, all ethnicities and religions are valued. (See Exhibit 7.1.)

Social Bridging: Strengthening Sense of Connection and Belonging to a Diverse Society

Social bridging, or connections to people who are unlike you in some important ways, is also important for refugee and immigrant youth (Almedom, 2005; Jasinskaja-Lahti et al., 2006). Social bridging allows youth to access services and information that might otherwise not be available to them. For example, a youth may form a relationship with students in her class who are familiar with and preparing for the college admissions process; as a result, she may become aware of the steps that she can take to prepare herself for college admission in the United States. At the wider level, adults and providers outside of the newly arrived community may have greater familiarity and access to resources, which they can extend to the refugee youth and

---

EXHIBIT 7.1. Key Questions About Social Bonds

- Does child/family express a sense of pride and connection with ethnic identity?
- Does family celebrate or practice aspects of their culture and religion?
  - If not, would they like to? What inhibits the ability to do so?
- Does child speak fluently in parents' native language?
  - If not, would they like to? What inhibits the ability to do so?
- Does the family participate in community events?
  - If not, would they like to? What inhibits their ability to do so?
- Does the physical environment of the office or therapeutic setting communicate openness to and value of diverse cultures?
  - If not, what can be done about it?

family through these bridging relationships. In this way, social bridging can be both an important part of a youth's developing identity as a part of America and a means of accessing different resources or experiences.

Refugee and immigrant children who live in families that are less acculturated into mainstream society may have relatively fewer avenues for crossing into diverse groups. Although schools are an important locus for integration, parents may not fully understand the value of after-school activities or may be hesitant to have their child engage in activities with which they are unfamiliar. Families with undocumented members may limit a child's involvement in community activities and events out of fear of deportation (Chavez, Lopez, Englebrecht, & Viramontez Anguiano, 2012). School- and community-based group-oriented activities can be important opportunities for social bridging: Sports, theater productions, music ensembles, community service, and a host of interest-based groups can provide structured and semistructured environments for youth to interact with other kids from various backgrounds and experiences. However, any offer or referral of youth to activities should be done with attention to the cultural heritage and immigration context and in consultation with the parents to avoid creating even more discord in a family that is already struggling with acculturative stress or fear of deportation. For instance, if Amira's parents felt strongly that she could not participate in a play if it required wearing Western attire but Amira was eager to participate, a therapist might try to address the conflict both by helping child and parent communicate their viewpoints, and by seeking involvement from the school around potential compromises. (See Exhibit 7.2.)

Social Linking: Strengthening Sense of Connection and Trust in Authority

As we have described before, a distrust of authority can be a legacy of the refugee and immigrant experience (Ellis, Miller, Baldwin, & Abdi, 2011).

EXHIBIT 7.2. Key Questions About Social Bridging

- Does child and/or family have regular, positive contact with members outside of their ethnic group?
  - If not, would they like to? What inhibits the ability to do so?
- Does child participate in community or school activities that include diverse youth?
  - If not, would they like to? What inhibits the ability to do so?
- Does the child have friends from different ethnic backgrounds, or the opportunity to meet people who are different from them?
  - If not, would they like to? What inhibits their ability to do so?

Yet receiving the protection and benefits afforded by the government, as well as community safety, necessitates that community members should feel comfortable and safe enough to turn to authorities. Although social linking may seem more remote to the therapeutic relationship than bonding and bridging, there are nonetheless important ways that therapists can support this connection. First and foremost, providers themselves represent authority figures. A stance of cultural humility, genuine connection and caring, and authentic relationship forms the foundation of trust between families and service systems. Beyond this, making an intentional effort to link families with appropriate services and supports (as described in Chapter 6) can also strengthen social linking. Finally, depending on the youth, there may be creative ways to help him or her feel engaged in, and an important part of, civil society in the new country. Civic engagement can be an important way for immigrant youth to experience a sense of mastery and identity in their community (Dixon, Bessaha, & Post, 2018). In a study of Latinx first- and second-generation 18-to-25-year-old immigrants of Dominican, Mexican, and Central American origin, many undocumented youth emerged as civic leaders, driven in part by social injustices related to legal status issues (Suárez-Orozco, Hernández, & Casanova, 2015). Supporting or encouraging civic or political engagement can convey to youth that their voices count and that a fundamental principle of democracy is the political equality of all citizens.

There may also be times when mental health providers can demonstrate their commitment to social justice by advocating against policies that are not in the best interest of refugee and immigrant children's well-being. Harmful practices such as holding asylum seekers in detention can undermine trust and connection with government; mental health professionals can help to counter this by taking a vocal stance advocating for more ethical and humane policies and practices. Examples of advocacy include sharing empirical evidence that shows that detention is harmful to the well-being of children, conducting research to further document these effects, and advocating at both an individual and systems level for the release of children currently being held in detention. (See Exhibit 7.3.)

RESILIENT COMMUNITIES: BEYOND THE THERAPEUTIC RELATIONSHIP

Think back to the initial story of Amira; her communities were resilient in ways that reached far deeper than a therapist's office. She encountered a supportive, inclusive school and a personable, helpful police officer. She had

EXHIBIT 7.3. Key Questions About Social Linking

- Does family experience therapeutic relationship as one of genuine respect?
- Does family experience support and genuine respect from providers of other services?
- Does family experience law enforcement as agents of protection and safety?
  - If not, is this based on past experiences of abuse in home country or current experiences of abuse or disrespect?
- Does family/youth engage civically and politically?
  - If not, would they like to? Are they aware of ways to do so?

friends who eagerly wanted to participate in her "fighting hatred" event, as well as a family and mosque that supported her interests. This sort of community resilience is built out of conscious efforts to encourage thoughtful, educated understanding of diverse experiences. Mental health providers can contribute to this broader resilience both as individual citizens and as trainers with specific expertise in promoting cultural responsivity and combating discrimination (Torres & Santiago, 2018). Trainings conducted for schools, law enforcement, or other systems can include basic principles of cultural humility, identity-affirming interventions, and trauma-informed care; at the end of this chapter a list of potential training topics is provided along with suggested resources to support mental health providers in conducting these trainings. Many of the community-outreach activities specified in Chapter 6 provide examples of building bridges and linkages between communities and systems.

Ultimately, we are not just mental health providers but also members of the diverse society that makes up this country. Similarly, refugees and immigrants are not just clients, but also neighbors and members of our communities. Their psychological well-being and resilience are affected not only by what happened in their past but also by what is happening right now in our schools, clinics, neighborhoods, and public institutions. We are collectively creating what kind of experiences will shape the development of refugee and immigrant youth. We are ambassadors for healing and resilience not only in our offices where we see patients but also across the social ecology. On a professional level, we can work to address the trauma and injustices refugees have experienced. On a personal level, we can work to fight social injustice in our communities and establish a place of safety, inclusion, and acceptance for all.

SAMPLE TRAINING TOPICS TO HELP BUILD MORE RESILIENT COMMUNITIES, AND ASSOCIATED RESOURCES

- The immigration/refugee experience:
  - *Crossroads: The Psychology of Immigration in the New Century*. Created by the APA Presidential Task Force on Immigration. Available from http://www.apa.org/topics/immigration/report.aspx
  - *Traumatic Separation and Refugee and Immigrant Children: Tips for Current Caregivers*. Available from https://www.nctsn.org/resources/traumatic-separation-and-refugee-and-immigrant-children-tips-current-caregivers

- Trauma 101: How trauma can affect youth:
  - *Age-Related Reactions to a Traumatic Event*. Describes how young children, school-age children, and adolescents react to traumatic events, and offers suggestions on how parents and caregivers can help and support them. Available from https://www.nctsn.org/resources/age-related-reactions-traumatic-event
  - *What is Child Traumatic Stress?* Defines child traumatic stress. This fact sheet gives an overview of trauma, describes traumatic stress symptoms, and ways children may be impacted. Available from https://www.nctsn.org/resources/what-child-traumatic-stress
  - *After a Crisis: Helping Young Children Heal*. Offers tips to parents on how to help young children, toddlers, and preschoolers heal after a traumatic event. Available from https://www.nctsn.org/resources/after-crisis-helping-young-children-heal

- Cultural humility:
  - Resources for providers and patients on topics related to multicultural psychology, available from https://multiculturalpsychology.com/
  - *Multicultural Guidelines: An Ecological Approach to Context, Identity and Intersectionality, 2017*. Available from https://www.apa.org/about/policy/multicultural-guidelines

- Cultural orientation related to specific immigrant/refugee groups:
  - Cultural Orientation Resource Center provides a collection of reports and videos on specific refugee cultural group. Available from http://www.culturalorientation.net/

- – Community cultural profiles and collection of related resources. Available from http://ethnomed.org/culture
- – Staff members of Ethnic Community-Based Organizations (ECBO; e.g., resettlement agency) who are from the community. For a primer on ECBOs, see https://www.migrationpolicy.org/research/bridging-divides-role-ethnic-community-based-organizations-refugee-integration

• Traumatic separation of refugee/immigrant families

- – Summary sheet of select NCTSN resources related to traumatic separation and refugee and immigrant trauma. Available from https://www.nctsn.org/sites/default/files/resources/fact-sheet/nctsn_resources_traumatic_separation_and_refugee_and_immigrant_trauma.pdf

- – NCTSN resource: *Guiding Caregivers: How to Talk to a Child About Deportation or Separation.* Available in English (https://www.nctsn.org/resources/guiding-caregivers-how-talk-child-about-deportation-or-separation) and Spanish (https://www.nctsn.org/resources/una-guia-para-los-cuidadores-como-hablarle-un-ninoa-sobre-la-deportacio-o-separacion).

References

Abdi, C. (2014). Threatened identities and gendered opportunities: Somali migration to America. *Signs: Journal of Women in Culture and Society, 39,* 459–483. http://dx.doi.org/10.1086/673380

Abdi, S. M., & Nisewaner, A. (2009). *Group work with Somali youth manual.* Unpublished manual, Refugee Trauma and Resilience Center at Boston Children's Hospital, Boston, MA.

Achenbach, T. M., & Rescorla, L. A. (2001). *Manual for the ASEBA School-Age Forms & Profiles.* Burlington: University of Vermont, Research Center for Children, Youth, & Families.

Adhikari, R., Benson, M., Nisewaner, A., & Abdi, S. M. (2013). *Group work with refugee youth: A group leader's manual.* Unpublished manual, Refugee Trauma and Resilience Center at Boston Children's Hospital, Boston, MA.

Alemi, Q., James, S., & Montgomery, S. (2016). Contextualizing Afghan refugee views of depression through narratives of trauma, resettlement stress, and coping. *Transcultural Psychiatry, 53,* 630–653. http://dx.doi.org/10.1177/1363461516660937

Allison, A. C., & Ferreira, R. J. (2017). Implementing cognitive behavioral intervention for trauma in schools (CBITS) with Latino youth. *Child and Adolescent Social Work Journal, 34,* 181–189. http://dx.doi.org/10.1007/s10560-016-0486-9

Almedom, A. M. (2005). Social capital and mental health: An interdisciplinary review of primary evidence. *Social Science & Medicine, 61,* 943–964. http://dx.doi.org/10.1016/j.socscimed.2004.12.025

Alvidrez, J. (1999). Ethnic variations in mental health attitudes and service use among low-income African American, Latina, and European American young women. *Community Mental Health Journal, 35,* 515–530. http://dx.doi.org/10.1023/A:1018759201290

American Psychiatric Association. (2013). *Diagnostic and statistical manual of mental disorders* (5th ed.). Arlington, VA: Author.

American Psychological Association. (2017). *Multicultural guidelines: An eco-logical approach to context, identity, and intersectionality.* Retrieved from https://www.apa.org/about/policy/multicultural-guidelines

American Psychological Association, Presidential Task Force on Evidence-Based Practice. (2006). Evidence-based practice in psychology. *American Psychologist, 61*, 271–285. http://dx.doi.org/10.1037/0003-066X.61.4.271

American Psychological Association, Presidential Task Force on Immigration. (2012). *Crossroads: The psychology of immigration in the new century.* Retrieved from http://www.apa.org/topics/immigration/report.aspx

Anguiano, R. M. (2018). Language brokering among Latino immigrant families: Moderating variables and youth outcomes. *Journal of Youth and Adolescence, 47*, 222–242. http://dx.doi.org/10.1007/s10964-017-0744-y

Apfel, R., & Simon, B. (1996). *Minefields in their hearts: The mental health of children in war.* New Haven, CT: Yale University Press.

Arora, P. G., Godoy, L., & Hodgkinson, S. (2017). Serving the underserved: Cultural considerations in behavioral health integration in pediatric primary care. *Professional Psychology: Research and Practice, 48*, 139–48. http://dx.doi.org/10.1037/pro0000131

Ayón, C. (2014). Service needs among Latino immigrant families: Implications for social work practice. *Social Work, 59*, 13–23. http://dx.doi.org/10.1093/sw/swt031

Baily, C. D., Henderson, S. W., & Tayler, R. (2016). Global mental health in our own backyard: An unaccompanied immigrant child's migration from El Salvador to New York City. *Journal of Clinical Psychology, 72*, 766–778. http://dx.doi.org/10.1002/jclp.22358

Banaji, M. R., & Greenwald, A. G. (2013). *Blindspot: Hidden biases of good people.* New York, NY: Delacorte Press.

Barrett, P. M., Moore, A. F., & Sonderegger, R. (2000). The FRIENDS program for young former-Yugoslavian refugees in Australia: A pilot study. *Behaviour Change, 17*, 124–133. http://dx.doi.org/10.1375/bech.17.3.124

Beck, A. T., Epstein, N., Brown, G., & Steer, R. A. (1988). An inventory for measuring clinical anxiety: Psychometric properties. *Journal of Consulting and Clinical Psychology, 56*, 893–897. http://dx.doi.org/10.1037/0022-006X.56.6.893

Beck, A. T., Steer, R. A., & Brown, G. K. (1996). *Beck Depression Inventory—II.* San Antonio, TX: The Psychological Corporation.

Beehler, S., Birman, D., & Campbell, R. (2012). The effectiveness of cultural adjustment and trauma services (CATS): Generating practice-based evidence on a comprehensive, school-based mental health intervention for immigrant youth. *American Journal of Community Psychology, 50*, 155–168. http://dx.doi.org/10.1007/s10464-011-9486-2

Behrens, D. (2017). *TST-R sustainability: Pulling the pieces together.* Unpublished report, Refugee Trauma and Resilience Center at Boston Children's Hospital, Boston, MA.

Beiser, M., & Hou, F. (2001). Language acquisition, unemployment and depressive disorder among Southeast Asian refugees: A 10-year study. *Social Science & Medicine, 53,* 1321–1334. http://dx.doi.org/10.1016/S0277-9536(00)00412-3

Benjet, C., Bromet, E., Karam, E. G., Kessler, R. C., McLaughlin, K. A., Ruscio, A. M., . . . Koenen, K. C. (2016). The epidemiology of traumatic event exposure worldwide: Results from the World Mental Health Survey Consortium. *Psychological Medicine, 46,* 327–343. http://dx.doi.org/10.1017/S0033291715001981

Berry, J. W. (2005). Acculturation: Living successfully in two cultures. *International Journal of Intercultural Relations, 29,* 697–712. http://dx.doi.org/10.1016/j.ijintrel.2005.07.013

Betancourt, J. R., Green, A. R., Carrillo, J. E., & Ananeh-Firempong, O., II. (2003). Defining cultural competence: A practical framework for addressing racial/ethnic disparities in health and health care. *Public Health Reports, 118,* 293–302. http://dx.doi.org/10.1016/S0033-3549(04)50253-4

Betancourt, T. S., Abdi, S., Ito, B. S., Lilienthal, G. M., Agalab, N., & Ellis, H. (2015). We left one war and came to another: Resource loss, acculturative stress, and caregiver–child relationships in Somali refugee families. *Cultural Diversity and Ethnic Minority Psychology, 21,* 114–125. http://dx.doi.org/10.1037/a0037538

Betancourt, T. S., Frounfelker, R., Mishra, T., Hussein, A., & Falzarano, R. (2015). Addressing health disparities in the mental health of refugee children and adolescents through community-based participatory research: A study in 2 communities. *American Journal of Public Health, 105,* S475–S482. http://dx.doi.org/10.2105/AJPH.2014.302504

Betancourt, T. S., Newnham, E. A., Birman, D., Lee, R., Ellis, B. H., & Layne, C. M. (2017). Comparing trauma exposure, mental health needs, and service utilization across clinical samples of refugee, immigrant, and U.S.-origin children. *Journal of Traumatic Stress, 30,* 209–218. http://dx.doi.org/10.1002/jts.22186

Bharadwaj, P., Pai, M. M., & Suziedelyte, A. (2017). Mental health stigma. *Economics Letters, 159,* 57–60. http://dx.doi.org/10.1016/j.econlet.2017.06.028

Birman, D., Ho, J., Pulley, E., Batia, K., Everson, M. L., Ellis, H., . . . Gonzalez, A. (2005). *Mental health interventions for refugee children in resettlement: White Paper II.* Washington, DC: National Child Traumatic Stress Network. Retrieved from https://www.nctsn.org/resources/mental-health-interventions-refugee-children-resettlement-white-paper-ii

Biswas, D., Kristiansen, M., Krasnik, A., & Norredam, M. (2011). Access to healthcare and alternative health-seeking strategies among undocumented migrants in Denmark. *BMC Public Health, 11,* 560. http://dx.doi.org/10.1186/1471-2458-11-560

Brabeck, K. M., Lykes, M. B., & Hunter, C. (2014). The psychosocial impact of detention and deportation on U.S. migrant children and families. *American Journal of Orthopsychiatry, 84*, 496–505. http://dx.doi.org/10.1037/ort0000011

Bronfenbrenner, U. (1979). *The ecology of human development: Experiments by nature and design.* Cambridge, MA: Harvard University Press.

Brown, J., Miller, J., & Mitchell, J. (2006). Interrupted schooling and the acquisition of literacy: Experiences of Sudanese refugees in Victorian secondary schools. *Australian Journal of Language and Literacy, 29*, 150–162.

Brownstein, J. N., Hirsch, G. R., Rosenthal, E. L., & Rush, C. H. (2011). Community health workers "101" for primary care providers and other stakeholders in health care systems. *The Journal of Ambulatory Care Management, 34*, 210–220. http://dx.doi.org/10.1097/JAC.0b013e31821c645d

Butler, P. D., Swift, M., Kothari, S., Nazeeri-Simmons, I., Friel, C. M., Longaker, M. T., & Britt, L. D. (2011). Integrating cultural competency and humility training into clinical clerkships: Surgery as a model. *Journal of Surgical Education, 68*, 222–230. http://dx.doi.org/10.1016/j.jsurg.2011.01.002

Cardeli, E., Phan, J., Mulder, L., Benson, M., Adhikari, R., & Ellis, B. H. (2019). *Bhutanese refugee youth: The importance of assessing and addressing psychosocial needs in a school setting.* Manuscript submitted for publication.

Casas, R., Guzmán-Vélez, E., Cardona-Rodriguez, J., Rodriguez, N., Quiñones, G., Izaguirre, B., & Tranel, D. (2012). Interpreter-mediated neuropsychological testing of monolingual Spanish speakers. *The Clinical Neuropsychologist, 26*, 88–101. http://dx.doi.org/10.1080/13854046.2011.640641

Cattell, R. B. (1963). Theory of fluid and crystallized intelligence: A critical experiment. *Journal of Educational Psychology, 54*, 1–22. http://dx.doi.org/10.1037/h0046743

Chan, C., Ying Ho, P. S., & Chow, E. (2002). A body-mind-spirit model in health: An Eastern approach. *Social Work in Health Care, 34*, 261–282. http://dx.doi.org/10.1300/J010v34n03_02

Chang, E. S., Simon, M., & Dong, X. (2012). Integrating cultural humility into health care professional education and training. *Advances in Health Sciences Education, 17*, 269–278. http://dx.doi.org/10.1007/s10459-010-9264-1

Chavez, J. M., Lopez, A., Englebrecht, C. M., & Viramontez Anguiano, R. P. (2012). *Sufren los niños*: Exploring the impact of unauthorized immigration status on children's well-being. *Family Court Review, 50*, 638–649. http://dx.doi.org/10.1111/j.1744-1617.2012.01482.x

Child Sexual Abuse Task Force and Research & Practice Core, National Child Traumatic Stress Network. (2004). *How to implement trauma-focused cognitive behavioral therapy.* Durham, NC, and Los Angeles, CA: National Center for Child Traumatic Stress.

Chudek, M., Cheung, B. Y., & Heine, S. J. (2015). U.S. immigrants' patterns of acculturation are sensitive to their age, language, and cultural contact but show no evidence of a sensitive window for acculturation. *Journal of Cognition and Culture, 15*, 174–190. http://dx.doi.org/10.1163/15685373-12342145

Cohen, J. A., & Kassan, A. (2018). Being in-between: A model of cultural identity negotiation for emerging adult immigrants. *Journal of Counseling Psychology, 65,* 133–154. http://dx.doi.org/10.1037/cou0000265

Cohen, J. A., Mannarino, A. P., & Deblinger, E. (2006). *Treating trauma and traumatic grief in children and adolescents.* New York, NY: Guilford Press.

Cohen, J. A., Mannarino, A. P., & Deblinger, E. (2017). *Treating trauma and traumatic grief in children and adolescents* (2nd ed.). New York, NY: Guilford Press.

Collie, P., Kindon, S., Liu, J., & Podsiadlowski, A. (2010). Mindful identity negotiations: The acculturation of young Assyrian women in New Zealand. *International Journal of Intercultural Relations, 34,* 208–220. http://dx.doi.org/10.1016/j.ijintrel.2009.08.002

Collier, L. (2015). Helping immigrant children heal. *Monitor on Psychology, 46,* 58. Retrieved from https://www.apa.org/monitor/2015/03/immigrant-children

Collier, V. P. (1995). Acquiring a second language for school. *Directions in Language and Education, 1,* 3–14.

Colucci, E., Minas, H., Szwarc, J., Guerra, C., & Paxton, G. (2015). In or out? Barriers and facilitators to refugee-background young people accessing mental health services. *Transcultural Psychiatry, 52,* 766–790. http://dx.doi.org/10.1177/1363461515571624

Colucci, E., Szwarc, J., Minas, H., Paxton, G., & Guerra, C. (2014). The utilisation of mental health services by children and young people from a refugee background: A systematic literature review. *International Journal of Culture and Mental Health, 7,* 86–108. http://dx.doi.org/10.1080/17542863.2012.713371

Copeland, W. E., Keeler, G., Angold, A., & Costello, E. J. (2007). Traumatic events and posttraumatic stress in childhood. *Archives of General Psychiatry, 64,* 577–584. http://dx.doi.org/10.1001/archpsyc.64.5.577

Corsetti, J. D. (2006). Marked for death: The Maras of Central America and those who flee their wrath. *Georgetown Immigration Law Journal, 20,* 407–435.

Courtois, C. A., & Gold, S. N. (2009). The need for inclusion of psychological trauma in the professional curriculum: A call to action. *Psychological Trauma: Theory, Research, Practice, and Policy, 1,* 3–23. http://dx.doi.org/10.1037/a0015224

Davidson, G. R., Murray, K. E., & Schweitzer, R. D. (2010). Review of refugee mental health assessment: Best practices and recommendations. *Journal of Pacific Rim Psychology, 4*(1), 72–85. http://dx.doi.org/10.1375/prp.4.1.72

Day-Vines, N. L., Wood, S. M., Grothaus, T., Craigen, L., Holman, A., Dotson-Blake, K., & Douglass, M. J. (2007). Broaching the subjects of race, ethnicity, and culture during the counseling process. *Journal of Counseling & Development, 85,* 401–409. http://dx.doi.org/10.1002/j.1556-6678.2007.tb00608.x

de Bruijn, B. (2009). *The living conditions and well-being of refugees*. St. Louis, MO: Federal Reserve Bank of St. Louis. Retrieved from http://hdr.undp.org/en/content/living-conditions-and-well-being-refugees

Dein, S., & Illaiee, A. S. (2013). Jinn and mental health: Looking at jinn possession in modern psychiatric practice. *The Psychiatrist, 37*, 290–293. http://dx.doi.org/10.1192/pb.bp.113.042721

DelVecchio Good, M. J., & Hannah, S. D. (2015). "Shattering culture": Perspectives on cultural competence and evidence-based practice in mental health services. *Transcultural Psychiatry, 52*, 198–221. http://dx.doi.org/10.1177/1363461514557348

DePrince, A., & Newman, E. (2011). Special issue editorial: The art and science of trauma-focused training and education. *Psychological Trauma: Theory, Research, Practice, and Policy, 3*, 213–214. http://dx.doi.org/10.1037/a0024640

Derluyn, I., Mels, C., & Broekaert, E. (2009). Mental health problems in separated refugee adolescents. *Journal of Adolescent Health, 44*, 291–297. http://dx.doi.org/10.1016/j.jadohealth.2008.07.016

diGrazia, B. (2018, March 21). Lynn community health center doctor looks out for refugees. *ItemLive*. Retrieved from https://www.itemlive.com/2018/03/21/lynn-community-health-center-doctor-looks-refugees/

Dimitry, L. (2012). A systematic review on the mental health of children and adolescents in areas of armed conflict in the Middle East. *Child: Care, Health and Development, 38*, 153–161. http://dx.doi.org/10.1111/j.1365-2214.2011.01246.x

Dixon, Z., Bessaha, M. L., & Post, M. (2018). Beyond the ballot: Immigrant integration through civic engagement and advocacy. *Race and Social Problems, 10*, 366–375. http://dx.doi.org/10.1007/s12552-018-9237-1

Dohan, D., & Schrag, D. (2005). Using navigators to improve care of underserved patients: Current practices and approaches. *Cancer, 104*, 848–855. http://dx.doi.org/10.1002/cncr.21214

Drew, N., Funk, M., Tang, S., Lamichhane, J., Chávez, E., Katontoka, S., . . . Saraceno, B. (2011). Human rights violations of people with mental and psychosocial disabilities: An unresolved global crisis. *The Lancet, 378*, 1664–1675. http://dx.doi.org/10.1016/S0140-6736(11)61458-X

Earner, I. (2007). Immigrant families and public child welfare: Barriers to services and approaches for change. *Child Welfare, 86*, 63–91.

Economic Services Administration. (n.d.). Refugee cash assistance. Retrieved from https://www.dshs.wa.gov/esa/community-services-offices/refugee-cash-assistance

Ehntholt, K. A., Smith, P. A., & Yule, W. (2005). School-based cognitive-behavioural therapy group intervention for refugee children who have experienced war-related trauma. *Clinical Child Psychology and Psychiatry, 10*, 235–250. http://dx.doi.org/10.1177/1359104505051214

Ellis, B. H., Ferris, S., Shattuck-Heidorn, H., Kim, C., & Elmore, D. (2018, May 10). *Exploring policy challenges, solutions, and resources for addressing trauma among refugee youth* [Webinar]. Retrieved from the National Child Traumatic Stress Network website: https://learn.nctsn.org/course/view.php?id=480

Ellis, B. H., Lincoln, A. K., Abdi, S. M., Nimmons, E. A., Issa, O., & Decker, S. H. (2018). "We all have stories": Black Muslim immigrants' experience with the police. *Race and Justice*. Advance online publication. http://dx.doi.org/10.1177/2153368718754638

Ellis, B. H., Lincoln, A. K., Charney, M. E., Ford-Paz, R., Benson, M., & Strunin, L. (2010). Mental health service utilization of Somali adolescents: Religion, community, and school as gateways to healing. *Transcultural Psychiatry, 47,* 789–811. http://dx.doi.org/10.1177/1363461510379933

Ellis, B. H., MacDonald, H. Z., Klunk-Gillis, J., Lincoln, A., Strunin, L., & Cabral, H. J. (2010). Discrimination and mental health among Somali refugee adolescents: The role of acculturation and gender. *American Journal of Orthopsychiatry, 80,* 564–575. http://dx.doi.org/10.1111/j.1939-0025.2010.01061.x

Ellis, B. H., MacDonald, H. Z., Lincoln, A. K., & Cabral, H. J. (2008). Mental health of Somali adolescent refugees: The role of trauma, stress, and perceived discrimination. *Journal of Consulting and Clinical Psychology, 76,* 184–193. http://dx.doi.org/10.1037/0022-006X.76.2.184

Ellis, B. H., Miller, A. B., Abdi, S., Barrett, C., Blood, E. A., & Betancourt, T. S. (2013). Multi-tier mental health program for refugee youth. *Journal of Consulting and Clinical Psychology, 81,* 129–140. http://dx.doi.org/10.1037/a0029844

Ellis, H. B., Miller, A. B., Baldwin, H., & Abdi, S. (2011). New directions in refugee youth mental health services: Overcoming barriers to engagement. *Journal of Child & Adolescent Trauma, 4,* 69–85. http://dx.doi.org/10.1080/19361521.2011.545047

Esala, J., Vukovich, M., Hanbury, A., Kashyap, S., & Joscelyne, A. (2018). Collaborative care for refugees and torture survivors: Key findings from the literature. *Traumatology, 24,* 168–185. Advance online publication. http://dx.doi.org/10.1037/trm0000143

Falicov, C. J. (2014). *Latino families in therapy* (2nd ed.). New York, NY: Guilford Press.

Fazel, M., Doll, H., & Stein, A. (2009). A school-based mental health intervention for refugee children: An exploratory study. *Clinical Child Psychology and Psychiatry, 14,* 297–309. http://dx.doi.org/10.1177/1359104508100128

Fazel, M., Garcia, J., & Stein, A. (2016). The right location? Experiences of refugee adolescents seen by school-based mental health services. *Clinical Child Psychology and Psychiatry, 21,* 368–380. http://dx.doi.org/10.1177/1359104516631606

Fazel, M., Karunakara, U., & Newnham, E. A. (2014). Detention, denial, and death: Migration hazards for refugee children. *The Lancet: Global Health, 2,* e313–e314. http://dx.doi.org/10.1016/S2214-109X(14)70225-6

Fazel, M., Reed, R. V., Panter-Brick, C., & Stein, A. (2012). Mental health of displaced and refugee children resettled in high-income countries: Risk and protective factors. *The Lancet, 379,* 266–282. http://dx.doi.org/10.1016/S0140-6736(11)60051-2

Fazel, M., & Stein, A. (2003). Mental health of refugee children: Comparative study. *BMJ: British Medical Journal, 327,* 134. http://dx.doi.org/10.1136/bmj.327.7407.134

Fitzsimons, E., Goodman, A., Kelly, E., & Smith, J. P. (2017). Poverty dynamics and parental mental health: Determinants of childhood mental health in the UK. *Social Science & Medicine, 175,* 43–51. http://dx.doi.org/10.1016/j.socscimed.2016.12.040

Fix, M., & Passel, J. S. (2002). *The scope and impact of welfare reform's immigrant provisions.* Retrieved from Urban Institute website: https://www.urban.org/sites/default/files/publication/60346/410412-Scope-and-Impact-of-Welfare-Reform-s-Immigrant-Provisions-The.PDF

Foronda, C., Baptiste, D. L., Reinholdt, M. M., & Ousman, K. (2016). Cultural humility: A concept analysis. *Journal of Transcultural Nursing, 27,* 210–217. http://dx.doi.org/10.1177/1043659615592677

Fox, P. G., Rossetti, J., Burns, K. R., & Popovich, J. (2005). Southeast Asian refugee children: A school-based mental health intervention. *The International Journal of Psychiatric Nursing Research, 11,* 1227–1236.

Fry, R., & Passel, J. S. (2009, May 28). *Latino children: A majority are U.S.-born offspring of immigrants.* Retrieved from Pew Research Center website: https://www.pewhispanic.org/2009/05/28/latino-children-a-majority-are-us-born-offspring-of-immigrants/

Fulginiti, L. C. (2008). Fatal footsteps: Murder of undocumented border crossers in Maricopa County, Arizona. *Journal of Forensic Sciences, 53,* 41–45. http://dx.doi.org/10.1111/j.1556-4029.2007.00613.x

Gadeberg, A. K., Montgomery, E., Frederiksen, H. W., & Norredam, M. (2017). Assessing trauma and mental health in refugee children and youth: A systematic review of validated screening and measurement tools. *European Journal of Public Health, 27,* 439–446. http://dx.doi.org/10.1093/eurpub/ckx034

Galliher, R. V., McLean, K. C., & Syed, M. (2017). An integrated developmental model for studying identity content in context. *Developmental Psychology, 53,* 2011–2022. http://dx.doi.org/10.1037/dev0000299

Gangsei, D., & Deutsch, A. C. (2007). Psychological evaluation of asylum seekers as a therapeutic process. *Torture, 17,* 79–87. Retrieved from https://www.ncbi.nlm.nih.gov/pubmed/17728485

Gans, H. (2009). First generation decline: Downward mobility among refugees and immigrants. *Ethnic and Racial Studies, 32,* 1658–1670. http://dx.doi.org/10.1080/01419870903204625

Girio-Herrera, E., & Owens, J. S. (2017). A pilot study examining a school-based parent engagement intervention following school mental health screening. *School Mental Health: A Multidisciplinary Research and Practice Journal, 9*, 117–131. http://dx.doi.org/10.1007/s12310-017-9208-5

Goodman, R., Meltzer, H., & Bailey, V. (1998). The strengths and difficulties questionnaire: A pilot study on the validity of the self-report version. *European Child & Adolescent Psychiatry, 7*, 125–130. http://dx.doi.org/10.1007/s007870050057

Greenfield, P. M. (1997). You can't take it with you: Why ability assessments don't cross cultures. *American Psychologist, 52*, 1115–1124. http://dx.doi.org/10.1037/0003-066X.52.10.1115

Gregg, J., & Saha, S. (2006). Losing culture on the way to competence: The use and misuse of culture in medical education. *Academic Medicine, 81*, 542–547. http://dx.doi.org/10.1097/01.ACM.0000225218.15207.30

Gregoire, J., Georgas, J., Saklofske, D. H., Van de Vijver, F., Wierzbicki, C., Weiss, L. G., & Zhu, J. (2008). Cultural issues in clinical use of WISC–IV. In A. Prifitera, D. H. Saklofske, & L. G. Weiss (Eds.), *WISC–IV clinical assessment and intervention* (pp. 495–522). San Diego, CA: Elsevier.

Griffiths, M. (2012). "Vile liars and truth distorters": Truth, trust, and the asylum system. *Anthropology Today, 28*(5), 8–12. http://dx.doi.org/10.1111/j.1467-8322.2012.00896.x

Grigg-Saito, D., Och, S., Liang, S., Toof, R., & Silka, L. (2008). Building on the strengths of a Cambodian refugee community through community-based outreach. *Health Promotion Practice, 9*, 415–425. http://dx.doi.org/10.1177/1524839906292176

Hacker, K., Chu, J., Leung, C., Marra, R., Pirie, A., Brahimi, M., . . . Marlin, R. P. (2011). The impact of Immigration and Customs Enforcement on immigrant health: Perceptions of immigrants in Everett, Massachusetts, USA. *Social Science & Medicine, 73*, 586–594. http://dx.doi.org/10.1016/j.socscimed.2011.06.007

Hadley, C., & Patil, C. (2009). Perceived discrimination among three groups of refugees resettled in the USA: Associations with language, time in the USA, and continent of origin. *Journal of Immigrant and Minority Health, 11*, 505–512. http://dx.doi.org/10.1007/s10903-009-9227-x

Halcón, L. L., Robertson, C. L., Savik, K., Johnson, D. R., Spring, M. A., Butcher, J. N., . . . Jaranson, J. M. (2004). Trauma and coping in Somali and Oromo refugee youth. *Journal of Adolescent Health, 35*, 17–25. http://dx.doi.org/10.1016/S1054-139X(03)00328-8

Haslam, S. A., Jetten, J., Postmes, T., & Haslam, C. (2009). Social identity, health and well-being: An emerging agenda for applied psychology. *Applied Psychology: An International Review, 58*, 1–23. http://dx.doi.org/10.1111/j.1464-0597.2008.00379.x

Hauck, F., Lo, E., Maxwell, A., & Reynolds, P. (2014). Factors influencing the acculturation of Burmese, Bhutanese, and Iraqi refugees into American society: Cross-cultural comparisons. *Journal of Immigrant & Refugee Studies*, *12*, 331–352. http://dx.doi.org/10.1080/15562948.2013.848007

Heath, N. M., Hall, B. J., Russ, E. U., Canetti, D., & Hobfoll, S. E. (2012). Reciprocal relationships between resource loss and psychological distress following exposure to political violence: An empirical investigation of COR theory's loss spirals. *Anxiety, Stress, and Coping: An International Journal*, *25*, 679–695. http://dx.doi.org/10.1080/10615806.2011.628988

Hecker, T., Fetz, S., Ainamani, H., & Elbert, T. (2015). The cycle of violence: Associations between exposure to violence, trauma-related symptoms, and aggression—findings from Congolese refugees in Uganda. *Journal of Traumatic Stress*, *28*, 448–455. http://dx.doi.org/10.1002/jts.22046

Hetherington, A. (2012). Supervision and the interpreting profession: Support and accountability through reflective practice. *International Journal of Interpreter Education*, *4*, 46–57.

Hodgkinson, S., Godoy, L., Beers, L. S., & Lewin, A. (2017). Improving mental health access for low-income children and families in the primary care setting. *Pediatrics*, *139*, e20151175. http://dx.doi.org/10.1542/peds.2015-1175

Holt-Lunstad, J., Smith, T. B., Baker, M., Harris, T., & Stephenson, D. (2015). Loneliness and social isolation as risk factors for mortality: A meta-analytic review. *Perspectives on Psychological Science*, *10*, 227–237. http://dx.doi.org/10.1177/1745691614568352

Hook, J. N. (2014). Engaging clients with cultural humility. *Journal of Psychology and Christianity*, *33*, 277–280.

Hoover, S. A., Sapere, H., Lang, J. M., Nadeem, E., Dean, K. L., & Vona, P. (2018). Statewide implementation of an evidence-based trauma intervention in schools. *School Psychology Quarterly*, *33*, 44–53. http://dx.doi.org/10.1037/spq0000248

Horvat, L., Horey, D., Romios, P., & Kis-Rigo, J. (2014). Cultural competence education for health professionals. *Cochrane Database of Systematic Reviews*, *10*, CD009405.

Hunt, X., & Swartz, L. (2017). Psychotherapy with a language interpreter: Considerations and cautions for practice. *South African Journal of Psychology*, *47*, 97–109. http://dx.doi.org/10.1177/0081246316650840

Hvass, A. M. F., & Wejse, C. (2017). Systematic health screening of refugees after resettlement in recipient countries: A scoping review. *Annals of Human Biology*, *44*, 475–483. http://dx.doi.org/10.1080/03014460.2017.1330897

Hynes, T. (2003). The issue of "trust" or "mistrust" in research with refugees: Choices, caveats and considerations for researchers. *New Issues in Refugee Research* [Working Paper No. 98]. Geneva, Switzerland: United Nations High Commissioner for Refugees.

Im, H., Ferguson, A., & Hunter, M. (2017). Cultural translation of refugee trauma: Cultural idioms of distress among Somali refugees in displacement. *Transcultural Psychiatry*, *54*, 626–652. http://dx.doi.org/10.1177/1363461517744989

Isakson, B. L., Legerski, J. P., & Layne, C. M. (2015). Adapting and implementing evidence-based interventions for trauma-exposed refugee youth and families. *Journal of Contemporary Psychotherapy, 45*, 245–253. http://dx.doi.org/10.1007/s10879-015-9304-5

Jasinskaja-Lahti, I., Liebkind, K., Jaakkola, M., & Reuter, A. (2006). Perceived discrimination, social support networks, and psychological well-being among three immigrant groups. *Journal of Cross-Cultural Psychology, 37*, 293–311. http://dx.doi.org/10.1177/0022022106286925

Jensen, L. A. (2010). Immigrant youth in the United States: Coming of age among diverse civic cultures. In L. Sherrod, J. Torney-Purta, & C. A. Flanagan (Eds.), *Handbook of research on civic engagement in youth* (pp. 425–443). Hoboken, NJ: Wiley. http://dx.doi.org/10.1002/9780470767603.ch16

Jezewski, M. A. (1990). Culture brokering in migrant farmworker health care. *Western Journal of Nursing Research, 12*, 497–513. http://dx.doi.org/10.1177/019394599001200406

Kaltman, S., Hurtado de Mendoza, A., Gonzales, F. A., Serrano, A., & Guarnaccia, P. J. (2011). Contextualizing the trauma experience of women immigrants from Central America, South America, and Mexico. *Journal of Traumatic Stress, 24*, 635–642. http://dx.doi.org/10.1002/jts.20698

Kaplan, I. (2009). Effects of trauma and the refugee experience on psychological assessment processes and interpretation. *Australian Psychologist, 44*, 6–15. http://dx.doi.org/10.1080/00050060802575715

Kaplan, I., Stolk, Y., Valibhoy, M., Tucker, A., & Baker, J. (2016). Cognitive assessment of refugee children: Effects of trauma and new language acquisition. *Transcultural Psychiatry, 53*, 81–109. http://dx.doi.org/10.1177/1363461515612933

Kataoka, S. H., Stein, B. D., Jaycox, L. H., Wong, M., Escudero, P., Tu, W., . . . Fink, A. (2003). A school-based mental health program for traumatized Latino immigrant children. *Journal of the American Academy of Child & Adolescent Psychiatry, 42*, 311–318. http://dx.doi.org/10.1097/00004583-200303000-00011

Keles, S., Friborg, O., Idsøe, T., Sirin, S., & Oppedal, B. (2018). Resilience and acculturation among unaccompanied refugee minors. *International Journal of Behavioral Development, 42*, 52–63. http://dx.doi.org/10.1177/0165025416658136

Keller, A., Joscelyne, A., Granski, M., & Rosenfeld, B. (2017). Pre-migration trauma exposure and mental health functioning among Central American migrants arriving at the US border. *PLoS One, 12*, e0168692. http://dx.doi.org/10.1371/journal.pone.0168692

Kenardy, J., Spence, S., & Macleod, A. (2006). Screening for posttraumatic stress disorder in children after accidental injury. *Pediatrics, 118*, 1002–1009. http://dx.doi.org/10.1542/peds.2006-0406

Kim, S. S., & Williams, D. R. (2012). Perceived discrimination and self-rated health in South Korea: A nationally representative survey. *PLoS One, 7*, e30501. http://dx.doi.org/10.1371/journal.pone.0030501

Kinzie, J. D., Sack, W., Angell, R., Clarke, G., & Ben, R. (1989). A three-year follow-up of Cambodian young people traumatized as children. *Journal of the American Academy of Child & Adolescent Psychiatry, 28*, 501–504. http://dx.doi.org/10.1097/00004583-198907000-00006

Kirmayer, L. J. (2012). Rethinking cultural competence. *Transcultural Psychiatry, 49*, 149–164. http://dx.doi.org/10.1177/1363461512444673

Kirmayer, L. J., Narasiah, L., Munoz, M., Rashid, M., Ryder, A. G., Guzder, J., . . . Pottie, K. (2011). Common mental health problems in immigrants and refugees: General approach in primary care. *Canadian Medical Association Journal, 183*, E959–E967. http://dx.doi.org/10.1503/cmaj.090292

Kleinman, A. (1980). Major conceptual and research issues for cultural (anthropological) psychiatry. *Culture, Medicine and Psychiatry, 4*(1), 3–13. http://dx.doi.org/10.1007/BF00051939

Kleinman, A. (1991). *Rethinking psychiatry*. New York, NY: Free Press.

Kleinman, A., Eisenberg, L., & Good, B. (2006). Culture, illness, and care: Clinical lessons from anthropologic and cross-cultural research. *Focus, 4*, 140–149. http://dx.doi.org/10.1176/foc.4.1.140

Kraft, C. (2018). *AAP statement opposing separation of children and parents at the border*. Retrieved from American Academy of Pediatrics website: https://www.aap.org/en-us/about-the-aap/aap-press-room/Pages/Statement OpposingSeparationofChildrenandParents.aspx

Kronick, R., Rousseau, C., & Cleveland, J. (2011). Mandatory detention of refugee children: A public health issue? *Paediatrics & Child Health, 16*, e65–e67.

Laban, C. J., Gernaat, H. B., Komproe, I. H., van der Tweel, I., & De Jong, J. T. (2005). Postmigration living problems and common psychiatric disorders in Iraqi asylum seekers in the Netherlands. *The Journal of Nervous and Mental Disease, 193*, 825–832. http://dx.doi.org/10.1097/01.nmd.0000188977.44657.1d

Layne, C. M., Olsen, J. A., Baker, A., Legerski, J.-P., Isakson, B., Pasalić, A., . . . Pynoos, R. S. (2010). Unpacking trauma exposure risk factors and differential pathways of influence: Predicting postwar mental distress in Bosnian adolescents. *Child Development, 81*, 1053–1076. http://dx.doi.org/10.1111/j.1467-8624.2010.01454.x

Li, S. S. Y., Liddell, B. J., & Nickerson, A. (2016). The relationship between post-migration stress and psychological disorders in refugees and asylum seekers. *Current Psychiatry Reports, 18*, 82. http://dx.doi.org/10.1007/s11920-016-0723-0

Lin, K. M., Fancher, T., & Cheung, F. (2010). Psychopharmacology for refugees and asylum seekers. In D. Bughra, T. Craig, & K. Bhui (Eds.), *Mental health of refugees and asylum seekers*. Oxford, England: Oxford University Press. http://dx.doi.org/10.1093/med/9780199557226.003.0011

Lindencrona, F., Ekblad, S., & Hauff, E. (2008). Mental health of recently resettled refugees from the Middle East in Sweden: The impact of pre-resettlement trauma, resettlement stress and capacity to handle stress. *Social Psychiatry and Psychiatric Epidemiology, 43*, 121–131. http://dx.doi.org/10.1007/s00127-007-0280-2

Lorek, A., Ehntholt, K., Nesbitt, A., Wey, E., Githinji, C., Rossor, E., & Wickramasinghe, R. (2009). The mental and physical health difficulties of children held within a British immigration detention center: A pilot study. *Child Abuse & Neglect, 33*, 573–585. http://dx.doi.org/10.1016/j.chiabu.2008.10.005

Lustig, S. L., Kia-Keating, M., Knight, W. G., Geltman, P., Ellis, H., Kinzie, J. D., . . . Saxe, G. N. (2004). Review of child and adolescent refugee mental health. *Journal of the American Academy of Child & Adolescent Psychiatry, 43*, 24–36. http://dx.doi.org/10.1097/00004583-200401000-00012

Madara, J. L. (2018, June 20). AMA urges administration to withdraw "zero tolerance" policy [Press release]. *American Medical Association.* Retrieved from https://www.ama-assn.org/press-center/press-release/ama-urges-administration-withdraw-zero-tolerance-policy

Mares, S. (2016). Fifteen years of detaining children who seek asylum in Australia—Evidence and consequences. *Australasian Psychiatry, 24*, 11–14. http://dx.doi.org/10.1177/1039856215620029

Mares, S., & Jureidini, J. (2004). Psychiatric assessment of children and families in immigration detention—Clinical, administrative and ethical issues. *Australian and New Zealand Journal of Public Health, 28*, 520–526. http://dx.doi.org/10.1111/j.1467-842X.2004.tb00041.x

Mares, S., Newman, L., Dudley, M., & Gale, F. (2002). Seeking refuge, losing hope: Parents and children in immigration detention. *Australasian Psychiatry, 10*, 91–96.

Masten, A. S., & Narayan, A. J. (2012). Child development in the context of disaster, war, and terrorism: Pathways of risk and resilience. *Annual Review of Psychology, 63*, 227–257. http://dx.doi.org/10.1146/annurev-psych-120710-100356

McCloskey, L. A., & Southwick, K. (1996). Psychosocial problems in refugee children exposed to war. *Pediatrics, 97*, 394–397.

Mena, F. J., Padilla, A. M., & Maldonado, M. (1987). Acculturative stress and specific coping strategies among immigrant and later generation college students. *Hispanic Journal of Behavioral Sciences, 9*, 207–225. http://dx.doi.org/10.1177/07399863870092006

Mendenhall, T. J., Kelleher, M. T., Baird, M. A., & Doherty, W. J. (2008). Overcoming depression in a strange land: A Hmong woman's journey in the world of Western medicine. In R. Kessler & D. Stafford (Eds.), *Collaborative medicine case studies: Evidence in practice* (pp. 327–340). New York, NY: Springer. http://dx.doi.org/10.1007/978-0-387-76894-6_27

Migration Policy Institute. (2014). *Profile of the unauthorized population: United States*. Retrieved from https://www.migrationpolicy.org/data/unauthorized-immigrant-population/state/US

Miletic, T., Piu, M., Minas, H., Stankovska, M., Stolk, Y., & Klimidis, S. (2006). *Guidelines for working effectively with interpreters in mental health settings*. Melbourne, Australia: Victorian Transcultural Psychiatry Unit.

Miller, K. E., Martell, Z. L., Pazdirek, L., Caruth, M., & Lopez, D. (2005). The role of interpreters in psychotherapy with refugees: An exploratory study. *American Journal of Orthopsychiatry, 75*, 27–39. http://dx.doi.org/10.1037/0002-9432.75.1.27

Mills, K. I. (2018, November 6). *APA decries proposal allowing indefinite detention of immigrant children* [Press release]. Retrieved from https://www.apa.org/news/press/releases/2018/11/detention-immigrant-children

Moitra, E., Duarte-Velez, Y., Lewis-Fernández, R., Weisberg, R. B., & Keller, M. B. (2018). Examination of *ataque de nervios* and *ataque de nervios* like events in a diverse sample of adults with anxiety disorders. *Depression and Anxiety, 35*, 1190–1197. http://dx.doi.org/10.1002/da.22853

Mollica, R. F., Caspi-Yavin, Y., Lavelle, J., Tor, S., Yang, T., Chan, S., . . . De Marneffe, D. (1996). Harvard Trauma Questionnaire (HTQ): Manual for Cambodian, Laotian and Vietnamese versions. *Torture, 6*, 19–33.

Mollica, R. F., Poole, C., Son, L., Murray, C. C., & Tor, S. (1997). Effects of war trauma on Cambodian refugee adolescents' functional health and mental health status. *Journal of the American Academy of Child & Adolescent Psychiatry, 36*, 1098–1106. http://dx.doi.org/10.1097/00004583-199708000-00017

Muñoz-Sandoval, A. F., Cummins, J., Alvarado, C. G., & Ruef, M. L. (2005). *Bilingual verbal ability tests—Normative update*. Rolling Meadows, IL: Riverside.

Murray, K. E., Davidson, G. R., & Schweitzer, R. D. (2010). Review of refugee mental health interventions following resettlement: Best practices and recommendations. *American Journal of Orthopsychiatry, 80*, 576–585. http://dx.doi.org/10.1111/j.1939-0025.2010.01062.x

Murray, L. K., Cohen, J. A., Ellis, B. H., & Mannarino, A. (2008). Cognitive behavioral therapy for symptoms of trauma and traumatic grief in refugee youth. *Child and Adolescent Psychiatric Clinics of North America, 17*, 585–604. http://dx.doi.org/10.1016/j.chc.2008.02.003

National Association of Social Workers. (2018, May 30). *NASW says plan to separate undocumented immigrant children from their parents is malicious and unconscionable* [Press release]. Retrieved from https://www.socialworkers.org/News/News-Releases/ID/1654/NASW-says-plan-to-separate-undocumented-immigrant-children-from-their-parents-is-malicious-and-unconscionable

National Center for Cultural Competence, Georgetown University Center for Child and Human Development, & Georgetown University Medical Center.

(2007). *Bridging the cultural divide in health care settings: The essential role of cultural broker programs.* Retrieved from https://nccc.georgetown.edu/culturalbroker/Cultural_Broker_EN.pdf

National Child Traumatic Stress Network. (2015). *Measures that are appropriate for refugee children and families.* Retrieved from https://www.nctsn.org/resources/measures-are-appropriate-refugee-children-and-families

Neuner, F., Catani, C., Ruf, M., Schauer, E., Schauer, M., & Elbert, T. (2008). Narrative exposure therapy for the treatment of traumatized children and adolescents (KidNET): From neurocognitive theory to field intervention. *Child and Adolescent Psychiatric Clinics of North America, 17,* 641–664. http://dx.doi.org/10.1016/j.chc.2008.03.001

Ngo, V., Langley, A., Kataoka, S. H., Nadeem, E., Escudero, P., & Stein, B. D. (2008). Providing evidence-based practice to ethnically diverse youths: Examples from the Cognitive Behavioral Intervention for Trauma in Schools (CBITS) program. *Journal of the American Academy of Child & Adolescent Psychiatry, 47,* 858–862. http://dx.doi.org/10.1097/CHI.0b013e3181799f19

Noels, K. A., & Clément, R. (2015). Situational variations in ethnic identity across immigration generations: Implications for acculturative change and cross-cultural adaptation. *International Journal of Psychology, 50,* 451–462. http://dx.doi.org/10.1002/ijop.12205

Noh, S., & Kaspar, V. (2003). Perceived discrimination and depression: Moderating effects of coping, acculturation, and ethnic support. *American Journal of Public Health, 93,* 232–238. http://dx.doi.org/10.2105/AJPH.93.2.232

Office of Refugee Resettlement. (2014). *Annual ORR report to congress—2005: Public/private partnerships.* Retrieved from https://www.acf.hhs.gov/orr/resource/annual-orr-report-to-congress-2005-public-private-partnerships

Otto, M. W., Hinton, D., Korbly, N. B., Chea, A., Ba, P., Gershuny, B. S., & Pollack, M. H. (2003). Treatment of pharmacotherapy-refractory post-traumatic stress disorder among Cambodian refugees: A pilot study of combination treatment with cognitive-behavior therapy vs sertraline alone. *Behaviour Research and Therapy, 41,* 1271–1276. http://dx.doi.org/10.1016/S0005-7967(03)00032-9

Papadopoulos, R. K. (2007). Refugees, trauma, and adversity-activated development. *European Journal of Psychotherapy & Counselling, 9,* 301–312. http://dx.doi.org/10.1080/13642530701496930

Parloff, M. B., Kelman, H. C., & Frank, J. D. (1954). Comfort, effectiveness, and self-awareness as criteria of improvement in psychotherapy. *The American Journal of Psychiatry, 111,* 343–352. http://dx.doi.org/10.1176/ajp.111.5.343

Pearlman, W. (2017). *We crossed a bridge and it trembled: Voices from Syria.* New York: HarperCollins.

Peek, C. J., & the National Integration Academy Council. (2013). *Lexicon for behavioral health and primary care integration: Concepts and definitions developed by expert consensus* (AHRQ Publication No.13-IP001-EF). Rockville, MD: Agency for Healthcare Research and Quality.

Perera, S., Gavian, M., Frazier, P., Johnson, D., Spring, M., Westermeyer, J., . . . Jaranson, J. (2013). A longitudinal study of demographic factors associated with stressors and symptoms in African refugees. *American Journal of Orthopsychiatry, 83*, 472–482. http://dx.doi.org/10.1111/ajop.12047

Pew Research Center. (2018, November 30). *Key findings about U.S. immigrants.* Retrieved from http://www.pewresearch.org/fact-tank/2018/09/14/key-findings-about-u-s-immigrants/

Physicians for Human Rights, & Bellevue/NYU Program for Survivors of Torture. (2003, June). *From persecution to prison: The health consequences of detention for asylum seekers.* Retrieved from https://phr.org/wp-content/uploads/2003/06/persecution-to-prison-US-2003.pdf

Poortinga, W. (2012). Community resilience and health: The role of bonding, bridging, and linking aspects of social capital. *Health & Place, 18*, 286–295. http://dx.doi.org/10.1016/j.healthplace.2011.09.017

Porter, M., & Haslam, N. (2005). Predisplacement and postdisplacement factors associated with mental health of refugees and internally displaced persons: A meta-analysis. *Journal of the American Medical Association, 294*, 610–612. http://dx.doi.org/10.1001/jama.294.5.602

Portland Public Schools. (2019). Demographic data. Retrieved from https://mlc.portlandschools.org/about/demographic_data

Procter, N. G., Kenny, M. A., Eaton, H., & Grech, C. (2018). Lethal hopelessness: Understanding and responding to asylum seeker distress and mental deterioration. *International Journal of Mental Health Nursing, 27*, 448–454. http://dx.doi.org/10.1111/inm.12325

Raval, H. (2005). Being heard and understood in the context of seeking asylum and refuge: Communicating with the help of bilingual co-workers. *Clinical Child Psychology and Psychiatry, 10*, 197–217. http://dx.doi.org/10.1177/1359104505051211

Raval, H., & Tribe, R. (2014). *Working with interpreters in mental health.* London, England: Routledge. http://dx.doi.org/10.4324/9781315812342

Rawlings, L. A., Capps, R., Gentsch, K., & Fortuny, K. (2007). *Immigrant integration into low-income urban neighborhoods.* Baltimore, MD: Annie E. Casey Foundation.

Razzouk, D., Nogueira, B., & Mari, J. J. (2011). A contribuição dos estudos transculturais dos países latino-americanos e caribenhos para a revisão da CID-10: Resultados preliminaries [The contribution of Latin American and Caribbean countries on culture bound syndromes studies for the CID-10 revision: Key findings from a work in progress]. *Brazilian Journal of Psychiatry, 33*, S5–S20. http://dx.doi.org/10.1590/S1516-44462011000500003

Rechtman, R. (2000). Stories of trauma and idioms of distress: From cultural narratives to clinical assessment. *Transcultural Psychiatry, 37*, 403–415. http://dx.doi.org/10.1177/136346150003700307

Refugee Trauma and Resilience Center. (2018). *Refugee Services Toolkit: Model of the four core stressors that contribute to refugee risk and resilience.* Retrieved from http://www.childrenshospital.org/centers-and-services/programs/o-_-z/refugee-trauma-and-resilience-center-program/training-and-resource-development

Reijneveld, S. A., de Boer, J. B., Bean, T., & Korfker, D. G. (2005). Unaccompanied adolescents seeking asylum: Poorer mental health under a restrictive reception. *The Journal of Nervous and Mental Disease, 193,* 759–761. http://dx.doi.org/10.1097/01.nmd.0000185870.55678.82

Robjant, K., & Fazel, M. (2010). The emerging evidence for Narrative Exposure Therapy: A review. *Clinical Psychology Review, 30,* 1030–1039. http://dx.doi.org/10.1016/j.cpr.2010.07.004

Romero, A. J., & Roberts, R. E. (2003). Stress within a bicultural context for adolescents of Mexican descent. *Cultural Diversity & Ethnic Minority Psychology, 9,* 171–184. http://dx.doi.org/10.1037/1099-9809.9.2.171

Rousseau, C. (1995). The mental health of refugee children. *Transcultural Psychiatry, 32,* 299–331. http://dx.doi.org/10.1177/136346159503200304

Rousseau, C. (2018). Addressing mental health needs of refugees. *The Canadian Journal of Psychiatry, 63,* 287–289. http://dx.doi.org/10.1177/0706743717746664

Rousseau, C., & Guzder, J. (2008). School-based prevention programs for refugee children. *Child and Adolescent Psychiatric Clinics of North America, 17,* 533–549, viii. http://dx.doi.org/10.1016/j.chc.2008.02.002

Rousseau, C., Measham, T., & Moro, M. R. (2011). Working with interpreters in child mental health. *Child and Adolescent Mental Health, 16,* 55–59. http://dx.doi.org/10.1111/j.1475-3588.2010.00589.x

Roxas, K., & Roy, L. (2012). "That's how we roll": A case study of a recently arrived refugee student in an urban high school. *The Urban Review, 44,* 468–486. http://dx.doi.org/10.1007/s11256-012-0203-8

Ruf, M., Schauer, M., Neuner, F., Catani, C., Schauer, E., & Elbert, T. (2010). Narrative exposure therapy for 7- to 16-year-olds: A randomized controlled trial with traumatized refugee children. *Journal of Traumatic Stress, 23,* 437–445. http://dx.doi.org/10.1002/jts.20548

Ruiz, E. (2016). Trauma symptoms in a diverse population of sexually abused children. *Psychological Trauma: Theory, Research, Practice, and Policy, 8,* 680–687. http://dx.doi.org/10.1037/tra0000160

Ryan, D., Dooley, B., & Benson, C. (2008). Theoretical perspectives on post-migration adaptation and psychological well-being among refugees: Towards a resource-based model. *Journal of Refugee Studies, 21,* 1–18. http://dx.doi.org/10.1093/jrs/fem047

Sanchez, A. L., Cornacchio, D., Poznanski, B., Golik, A. M., Chou, T., & Comer, J. S. (2018). The effectiveness of school-based mental health services for elementary-aged children: A meta-analysis. *Journal of the American Academy* of Child & Adolescent Psychiatry, 57, 153–165. http://dx.doi.org/10.1016/j.jaac.2017.11.022

Sangalang, C. C., Jager, J., & Harachi, T. W. (2017). Effects of maternal traumatic distress on family functioning and child mental health: An examination of Southeast Asian refugee families in the U.S. Social Science & Medicine, 184, 178–186. http://dx.doi.org/10.1016/j.socscimed.2017.04.032

Santiago, C. D., Raviv, T., & Jaycox, L. (2018). Creating healing school communities: School-based interventions for students exposed to trauma. Washington, DC: American Psychological Association.

Saxe, G., Ellis, B. H., & Brown, A. D. (2015). Trauma systems therapy for children and teens (2nd ed.). New York, NY: Guilford Press.

Saxe, G. N., Ellis, B. H., & Kaplow, J. B. (2007). Collaborative treatment of traumatized children and teens: The trauma systems therapy approach. New York, NY: Guilford Press.

Schilling, S., Fortin, K., & Forkey, H. (2015). Medical management and trauma-informed care for children in foster care. Current Problems in Pediatric and Adolescent Health Care, 45, 298–305. http://dx.doi.org/10.1016/j.cppeds.2015.08.004

Schock, K., Rosner, R., & Knaevelsrud, C. (2015). Impact of asylum interviews on the mental health of traumatized asylum seekers. European Journal of Psychotraumatology, 6, 26286. http://dx.doi.org/10.3402/ejpt.v6.26286

Schwartz, S. J., Unger, J. B., Zamboanga, B. L., & Szapocznik, J. (2010). Rethinking the concept of acculturation: Implications for theory and research. American Psychologist, 65, 237–251. http://dx.doi.org/10.1037/a0019330

Schweitzer, R., Melville, F., Steel, Z., & Lacherez, P. (2006). Trauma, post-migration living difficulties, and social support as predictors of psychological adjustment in resettled Sudanese refugees. Australian and New Zealand Journal of Psychiatry, 40, 179–187. http://dx.doi.org/10.1080/j.1440-1614.2006.01766.x

Scuglik, D. L., Alarcón, R. D., Lapeyre, A. C., III, Williams, M. D., & Logan, K. M. (2007). When the poetry no longer rhymes: Mental health issues among Somali immigrants in the USA. Transcultural Psychiatry, 44, 581–595. http://dx.doi.org/10.1177/1363461507083899

Searight, H. R., & Searight, B. K. (2009). Working with foreign language interpreters: Recommendations for psychological practice. Professional Psychology: Research and Practice, 40, 444–451. http://dx.doi.org/10.1037/a0016788

Shannon, P. J., Wieling, E., Simmelink-McCleary, J., & Becher, E. (2015). Beyond stigma: Barriers to discussing mental health in refugee populations. Journal of Loss and Trauma, 20, 281–296. http://dx.doi.org/10.1080/15325024.2014.934629

Shim, R., & Rust, G. (2013). Primary care, behavioral health, and public health: Partners in reducing mental health stigma. American Journal of Public Health, 103, 774–776. http://dx.doi.org/10.2105/AJPH.2013.301214

Silove, D., Austin, P., & Steel, Z. (2007). No refuge from terror: The impact of detention on the mental health of trauma-affected refugees seeking asylum in Australia. *Transcultural Psychiatry, 44,* 359–393. http://dx.doi.org/10.1177/1363461507081637

Silove, D., Sinnerbrink, I., Field, A., Manicavasagar, V., & Steel, Z. (1997). Anxiety, depression and PTSD in asylum-seekers: Associations with pre-migration trauma and post-migration stressors. *British Journal of Psychiatry, 170,* 351–357. http://dx.doi.org/10.1192/bjp.170.4.351

Singh, N. N., McKay, J. D., & Singh, A. N. (1999). The need for cultural brokers in mental health services. *Journal of Child and Family Studies, 8,* 1–10. http://dx.doi.org/10.1023/A:1022949225965

Sleijpen, M., Haagen, J., Mooren, T., & Kleber, R. J. (2016). Growing from experience: An exploratory study of posttraumatic growth in adolescent refugees. *European Journal of Psychotraumatology, 7,* 28698. http://dx.doi.org/10.3402/ejpt.v7.28698

Smajkic, A., Weine, S., Djuric-Bijedic, Z., Boskailo, E., Lewis, J., & Pavkovic, I. (2001). Sertraline, paroxetine, and venlafaxine in refugee posttraumatic stress disorder with depression symptoms. *Journal of Traumatic Stress, 14,* 445–452. http://dx.doi.org/10.1023/A:1011177420069

Sonne, C., Carlsson, J., Bech, P., Elklit, A., & Mortensen, E. L. (2016). Treatment of trauma-affected refugees with venlafaxine versus sertraline combined with psychotherapy—A randomised study. *BMC Psychiatry, 16,* 383. http://dx.doi.org/10.1186/s12888-016-1081-5

Sonne, C., Carlsson, J., Bech, P., & Mortensen, E. L. (2017). Pharmacological treatment of refugees with trauma-related disorders: What do we know today? *Transcultural Psychiatry, 54,* 260–280. http://dx.doi.org/10.1177/1363461516682180

Sousa, V. D., & Rojjanasrirat, W. (2011). Translation, adaptation and validation of instruments or scales for use in cross-cultural health care research: A clear and user-friendly guideline. *Journal of Evaluation in Clinical Practice, 17,* 268–274. http://dx.doi.org/10.1111/j.1365-2753.2010.01434.x

Spitzer, R. L., Kroenke, K., Williams, J. B. W., & the Patient Health Questionnaire Primary Care Study Group. (1999). Validation and utility of a self-report version of PRIME-MD: The PHQ primary care study. *JAMA, 282,* 1737–1744. http://dx.doi.org/10.1001/jama.282.18.1737

Steel, Z., Momartin, S., Bateman, C., Hafshejani, A., Silove, D. M., Everson, N., . . . Mares, S. (2004). Psychiatric status of asylum seeker families held for a protracted period in a remote detention centre in Australia. *Australian and New Zealand Journal of Public Health, 28,* 527–536.

Steele, C. M. (1997). A threat in the air: How stereotypes shape intellectual identity and performance. *American Psychologist, 52,* 613–629. http://dx.doi.org/10.1037/0003-066X.52.6.613

Steele, C. M. (2010). *Whistling Vivaldi: And other clues to how stereotypes affect us.* New York, NY: W. W. Norton.

Steinberg, A. M., Brymer, M., Decker, K., & Pynoos, R. S. (2004). The University of California at Los Angeles post-traumatic stress disorder reaction index. *Current Psychiatry Reports*, *6*, 96–100. http://dx.doi.org/10.1007/s11920-004-0048-2

Stepick, A., & Stepick, C. D. (2002). Becoming American, constructing ethnicity: Immigrant youth and civic engagement. *Applied Developmental Science*, *6*, 246–257. http://dx.doi.org/10.1207/S1532480XADS0604_12

Suárez-Orozco, C., Bang, H. J., & Kim, H. Y. (2011). I felt like my heart was staying behind: Psychological implications of family separations and reunifications for immigrant youth. *Journal of Adolescent Research*, *26*, 222–257. http://dx.doi.org/10.1177/0743558410376830

Suárez-Orozco, C., Hernández, M. G., & Casanova, S. (2015). "It's sort of my calling": The civic engagement and social responsibility of Latino immigrant-origin young adults. *Research in Human Development*, *12*, 84–99. http://dx.doi.org/10.1080/15427609.2015.1010350

Sue, D. W., Capodilupo, C. M., Torino, G. C., Bucceri, J. M., Holder, A. M. B., Nadal, K. L., & Esquilin, M. (2007). Racial microaggressions in everyday life: Implications for clinical practice. *American Psychologist*, *62*, 271–286. http://dx.doi.org/10.1037/0003-066X.62.4.271

Sue, D. W., & Sue, D. (2015). *Counseling the culturally diverse: Theory and practice* (6th ed.). Hoboken, NJ: John Wiley & Sons.

Sue, D. W., & Sue, D. (2017). *Counseling the culturally diverse: Theory and practice* (7th ed.). Hoboken, NJ: John Wiley & Sons.

Sullivan, A., & Simonson, G. R. (2016). A systematic review of school-based social-emotional interventions for refugee and war-traumatized youth. *Review of Educational Research*, *86*, 503–530. http://dx.doi.org/10.3102/0034654315609419

Summerfield, D. (1999). A critique of seven assumptions behind psychological trauma programmes in war-affected areas. *Social Science & Medicine*, *48*, 1449–1462. http://dx.doi.org/10.1016/S0277-9536(98)00450-X

Suzuki, L. A., & Ponterotto, J. G. (Eds.). (2008). *Handbook of multicultural assessment: Clinical, psychological, and educational applications*. San Francisco, CA: Jossey-Bass.

Tay, A. K., Rees, S., Chen, J., Kareth, M., Mohsin, M., & Silove, D. (2015). The Refugee-Mental Health Assessment Package (R-MHAP): Rationale, development and first-stage testing amongst West Papuan refugees. *International Journal of Mental Health Systems*, *9*, 1–13. http://dx.doi.org/10.1186/s13033-015-0018-6

Telzer, E. H. (2010). Expanding the acculturation gap-distress model: An integrative review of research. *Human Development*, *53*, 313–340. http://dx.doi.org/10.1159/000322476

Teodorescu, D. S., Heir, T., Hauff, E., Wentzel-Larsen, T., & Lien, L. (2012). Mental health problems and post-migration stress among multi-traumatized refugees attending outpatient clinics upon resettlement to Norway. *Scandinavian Journal of Psychology, 53,* 316–332. http://dx.doi.org/10.1111/j.1467-9450.2012.00954.x

Tervalon, M., & Murray-García, J. (1998). Cultural humility versus cultural competence: A critical distinction in defining physician training outcomes in multicultural education. *Journal of Health Care for the Poor and Underserved, 9,* 117–125. http://dx.doi.org/10.1353/hpu.2010.0233

Thackrah, R. D., & Thompson, S. C. (2013). Refining the concept of cultural competence: Building on decades of progress. *The Medical Journal of Australia, 199,* 35–38. http://dx.doi.org/10.5694/mja13.10499

Torres, S. A., & Santiago, C. D. (2018). Stress and cultural resilience among low-income Latino adolescents: Impact on daily mood. *Cultural Diversity & Ethnic Minority Psychology, 24,* 209–220. http://dx.doi.org/10.1037/cdp0000179

Torres, S. A., Santiago, C. D., Walts, K. K., & Richards, M. H. (2018). Immigration policy, practices, and procedures: The impact on the mental health of Mexican and Central American youth and families. *American Psychologist, 73,* 843–854. http://dx.doi.org/10.1037/amp0000184

Torres Fernández, I., Chavez-Dueñas, N., & Consoli, A. (2015). Guidelines for mental health professionals working with unaccompanied asylum-seeking minors. *Latina/o. Psychology Today, 2,* 44–54.

Tribe, R., & Lane, P. (2009). Working with interpreters across language and culture in mental health. *Journal of Mental Health, 18,* 233–241. http://dx.doi.org/10.1080/09638230701879102

Tyrer, R. A., & Fazel, M. (2014). School and community-based interventions for refugee and asylum seeking children: A systematic review. *PLoS One, 9,* e89359. http://dx.doi.org/10.1371/journal.pone.0089359

Ungar, M., & Liebenberg, L. (2011). Assessing resilience across cultures using mixed methods: Construction of the child and youth resilience measure. *Journal of Mixed Methods Research, 5,* 126–149. http://dx.doi.org/10.1177/1558689811400607

United Nations High Commissioner for Refugees. (1951). *Convention and protocol relating to the status of refugees.* New York, NY: Communications and Public Information Service.

United Nations High Commissioner for Refugees. (2014, March 12). *Children on the run.* Retrieved from http://www.unhcr.org/en-us/children-on-the-run.html

United Nations High Commissioner for Refugees. (2017, September 12). *UNHCR report highlights education crisis for refugee children.* Retrieved from http://www.unhcr.org/en-us/news/press/2017/9/59b6a3ec4/unhcr-report-highlights-education-crisis-refugee-children.html

United Nations High Commissioner for Refugees. (2018a). *Global trends: Forced displacement in 2017.* Retrieved from https://www.unhcr.org/en-us/statistics/unhcrstats/5b27be547/unhcr-global-trends-2017.html

United Nations High Commissioner for Refugees. (2018b). *U.S. resettlement facts*. Retrieved from http://www.unhcr.org/en-us/us-refugee-resettlement-facts.html

Unterhitzenberger, J., Eberle-Sejari, R., Rassenhofer, M., Sukale, T., Rosner, R., & Goldbeck, L. (2015). Trauma-focused cognitive behavioral therapy with unaccompanied refugee minors: A case series. *BMC Psychiatry, 15*, 260–269. http://dx.doi.org/10.1186/s12888-015-0645-0

U.S. Citizenship and Immigration Services. (2019). *Asylum*. Retrieved from https://www.uscis.gov/humanitarian/refugees-asylum/asylum

U.S. Government Accountability Office. (2010). *Iraqi refugees and special immigrant visa holders face challenges resettling in the United States and obtaining U.S. government employment*. Retrieved from http://www.gao.gov/new.items/d10274.pdf

Veliu, B., & Leathem, J. (2017). Neuropsychological assessment of refugees: Methodological and cross-cultural barriers. *Applied Neuropsychology: Adult, 24*, 481–492. http://dx.doi.org/10.1080/23279095.2016.1201483

Vinokurov, A., Trickett, E. J., & Birman, D. (2002). Acculturative hassles and immigrant adolescents: A life-domain assessment for Soviet Jewish refugees. *The Journal of Social Psychology, 142*, 425–445. http://dx.doi.org/10.1080/00224540209603910

von Werthern, M., Robjant, K., Chui, Z., Schon, R., Ottisova, L., Mason, C., & Katona, C. (2018). The impact of immigration detention on mental health: A systematic review. *BMC Psychiatry, 18*, 382–401. http://dx.doi.org/10.1186/s12888-018-1945-y

Walsh, F. (2007). Traumatic loss and major disasters: Strengthening family and community resilience. *Family Process, 46*, 207–227. http://dx.doi.org/10.1111/j.1545-5300.2007.00205.x

Waters, M. C. (1994). Ethnic identities of second-generation black immigrants in New York City. *International Migration Review, 28*, 795–820. http://dx.doi.org/10.1177/019791839402800408

Wechsler, D. (2014). *WISC–V: Technical and Interpretive Manual*. Bloomington, MN: Pearson.

Weine, S. M. (2008). Family roles in refugee youth resettlement from a prevention perspective. *Child and Adolescent Psychiatric Clinics of North America, 17*, 515–532, vii–viii. http://dx.doi.org/10.1016/j.chc.2008.02.006

Weine, S. M. (2011). Developing preventive mental health interventions for refugee families in resettlement. *Family Process, 50*, 410–430. http://dx.doi.org/10.1111/j.1545-5300.2011.01366.x

Weine, S. M. (2015). Family roles in refugee youth resettlement from a prevention perspective. *Child and Adolescent Psychiatric Clinics of North America, 25*, 713–724.

Westermeyer, J. J., Campbell, R., Lien, R., Spring, M., Johnson, D. R., Butcher, J., . . . Jaranson, J. M. (2010). HADStress: A somatic symptom screen for posttraumatic stress among Somali refugees. *Psychiatric Services*, *61*, 1132–1137. http://dx.doi.org/10.1176/ps.2010.61.11.1132

Williams, D. R., & Mohammed, S. A. (2009). Discrimination and racial disparities in health: Evidence and needed research. *Journal of Behavioral Medicine*, *32*, 20–47. http://dx.doi.org/10.1007/s10865-008-9185-0

Williams, D. R., Yu, Y., Jackson, J. S., & Anderson, N. B. (1997). Racial differences in physical and mental health: Socio-economic status, stress and discrimination. *Journal of Health Psychology*, *2*, 335–351. http://dx.doi.org/10.1177/135910539700200305

Winer, J. P., Issa, O., Park, H. S., Nisewaner, A., & Abdi, S. M. (2018). *Promoting resilience in Somali-Canadian adolescents: A group leader's manual.* Unpublished manual, Refugee Trauma and Resilience Center at Boston Children's Hospital, Boston, MA.

Witmer, A., Seifer, S. D., Finocchio, L., Leslie, J., & O'Neil, E. H. (1995). Community health workers: Integral members of the health care work force. *American Journal of Public Health*, *85*, 1055–1058. http://dx.doi.org/10.2105/AJPH.85.8_Pt_1.1055

Wood, L. C. N. (2018). Impact of punitive immigration policies, parent-child separation and child detention on the mental health and development of children. *BMJ Paediatrics Open*, *2*, e000338. http://dx.doi.org/10.1136/bmjpo-2018-000338

Zong, J., Batalova, J., & Burrows, M. (2019, March 14). *Frequently requested statistics on immigrants and immigration in the United States.* Retrieved from Migration Policy Institute website: https://www.migrationpolicy.org/article/frequently-requested-statistics-immigrants-and-immigration-united-states

Index

About the Authors

B. Heidi Ellis, PhD, is an associate professor of psychology in the Department of Psychiatry at Harvard Medical School and Boston Children's Hospital, and a licensed clinical psychologist. She is also the director of the Refugee Trauma and Resilience Center at Boston Children's Hospital, a partner in the National Child Traumatic Stress Network. She received a BA from Yale University and a PhD in clinical psychology from the University of Oregon. Dr. Ellis's primary focus is on understanding and promoting refugee youth mental health and well-being, with a particular emphasis on understanding how trauma exposure, violence, and social context impact developmental trajectories. Over the past 17 years she has conducted a community-based participatory research program with Somali youth; she is currently principal investigator of a multisite, longitudinal research project examining developmental pathways to and away from violence. Dr. Ellis is also codeveloper of the trauma treatment model, trauma systems therapy, and the 2018 recipient of the Sarah Haley Award for Clinical Excellence from the International Society for Traumatic Stress Studies.

Saida M. Abdi, PhD, is an assistant professor in the School of Social Work in the College of Education and Human Development at the University of Minnesota. Dr. Abdi received a combined social work/sociology PhD from Boston University. Prior to her position at the University of Minnesota, she was the associate director for community relations at the Boston Children's Hospital Refugee Trauma and Resilience Center (RTRC). In this role, she has led RTRC's efforts to build community partnerships and to increase mental health knowledge and services in diverse refugee communities. Her clinical practice focuses on supporting children and families impacted by violence and migration and her research focuses on factors related to resilience among refugee and immigrant children and families and the use of community-based participatory research to promote community engagement and collaboration. She is a cofounder clinician at the Refugee and Immigrant Assistance Center, which was created by refugees and immigrants to meet the mental health needs of refugees and immigrants. She is principal investigator of a multisite impact evaluation of trauma systems therapy for refugees in Canada.

Jeffrey P. Winer, PhD, is an attending psychologist at the Refugee Trauma and Resilience Center at Boston Children's Hospital and an instructor of psychology in the Department of Psychiatry at Harvard Medical School. Dr. Winer's work is primarily focused on developing, testing, disseminating, and implementing culturally responsive psychological interventions for youth and families of refugee and immigrant backgrounds. He is an active researcher, clinician, educator, and consultant, and is the recipient of a Thrasher Research Fund Early Career Award. Dr. Winer received his undergraduate degree from Grinnell College and his MS and PhD in clinical psychology from the University of Massachusetts Amherst. He completed his clinical internship at McLean Hospital/Harvard Medical School and his postdoctoral fellowship at Boston Children's Hospital/Harvard Medical School. Outside of his work at Boston Children's Hospital, he continues to work at the McLean Hospital 3East Adolescent DBT Partial Hospital Program and maintains a private practice.